D1363637

The Little Guide to Getting Your Book Published

Simple Steps to Success

John Bond

ROWMAN & LITTLEFIELD
Lanham • Boulder • New York • London

Published by Rowman & Littlefield
An imprint of The Rowman & Littlefield Publishing Group, Inc.
4501 Forbes Boulevard, Suite 200, Lanham, Maryland 20706
www.rowman.com

86-90 Paul Street, London EC2A 4NE, United Kingdom

British Library Cataloguing in Publication Information Available

Library of Congress Cataloging-in-Publication Data

Names: Bond, John, 1960– author.
Title: The little guide to getting your book published : simple steps to success / John Bond.
Description: Lanham : Rowman & Littlefield, [2023] | Includes bibliographical references and index. | Summary: "The Little Guide to Getting Your Book Published takes prospective authors from idea to draft manuscript to published book in a step-by-step process"— Provided by publisher.
Identifiers: LCCN 2023019685 (print) | LCCN 2023019686 (ebook) | ISBN 9781475870176 (paperback) | ISBN 9781475870183 (epub)
Subjects: LCSH: Authorship—Marketing. | Authorship.
Classification: LCC PN161 .B65 2023 (print) | LCC PN161 (ebook) | DDC 808.3—dc23/eng/20230503
LC record available at https://lccn.loc.gov/2023019685
LC ebook record available at https://lccn.loc.gov/2023019686

♾️™ The paper used in this publication meets the minimum requirements of American National Standard for Information Sciences—Permanence of Paper for Printed Library Materials, ANSI/NISO Z39.48-1992.

This book is dedicated to all of the people in my life that have helped me develop my deep love of books and the written word. Its origins can be traced back to a confluence of influences: Connie Bond, the Langhorne Library and Harriet Pickel, Stanley Orkis, Slatoff Auctions and Oliver Wendell Holmes, Thomas Merton, Ray Bradbury, and many others. They ushered me into a world full of immense knowledge and adventure.

Contents

Foreword

A Detailed Road Map

John Bond has written a "Must-Have" resource for people who are thinking about writing a book, individuals who are immersed in the writing process, and published authors.

I think of this book as "Required Reading" before people begin to write their manuscript and throughout their writing process. John offers novice and veteran writers a detailed road map to reach their goals with proven, educational, and enlightening stops along the way to make the journey easier to successfully reach an author's goals and complete their authorship adventure.

If a writer embarks on an authorship adventure, an accurate and fact-filled guidebook written by a publishing expert is advisable. If he or she runs into a dead-end quandary, the solution will be within the pages of John's book, and his publishing wisdom will guide them back to the correct writing path.

John's expertise will help writers answer the following, sometimes daunting, questions:

- Can I really become a published author?
- What do I need to know before I write my book?
- Are there different ways that my book can be published?
- Will I be able to understand the mysterious book publishing process?
- What methods should I use to market and promote my book?
- Who should I ask for professional advice?

John's publishing experiences qualify him as a proficient guide who knows the direct routes and detours that will save invaluable time and effort. John has over twenty-five years in publishing as an editor and then as publisher. He has been the publisher for over 500 titles and has written six books himself.

Now, John is a quintessential publishing consultant because he has also spoken with hundreds of people about guiding them along the path to becoming published authors.

I am confident you will enjoy the privilege and appreciate the gifts of John's wisdom and his essential book publishing information as you embark on your authorship adventure to write and publish your book successfully!

Sheila N. Glazov
What Color Is Your Brain? A Fun and Fascinating Approach to Understanding Yourself and Others (Thorofare, NJ: SLACK, 2008)
Best-selling author, internationally known professional speaker, personality expert, and passionate educator
www.sheilaglazov.com

Preface

Helping Authors Get Their Books Published

Publishing a book is easier to accomplish then in any previous time. Part of this has to do with hybrid and self-publishing, but also the proliferation of options available in the digital age. Having said this, authors still face the issues of finding a publisher or agent with trepidation. If you want to find a big New York publisher that will pay you an advance to write the book and then have your book appear everywhere, all at once, the mountain remains as steep and foreboding as ever.

Education is key to getting started and perseverance is essential to success. I am here to tell you the mountain can be climbed successfully, but the exact destination and route are not guaranteed.

I have worked with key figures in their field as well as students just getting started. Many have been based in North America and Europe, but also in India, Saudi Arabia, and Vietnam. They all share one thing in common: the desire to be published book authors.

I have worked for over thirty years in scholarly publishing: as an editor, publisher, chief content officer, author, mentor, and writing and publishing consultant. See the "About the Author" section at the end of the book to learn more about my background including my YouTube channel (which has over one hundred videos on publishing topics you might find of interest). I have overseen the publishing of 500 books and 20,000 journal articles in my career and have written six books myself. My most recent are companions to this one: *The Little Guide to Getting Your Journal Article Published* and *The Little Guide to Giving Poster Presentations.*

I decided to write this book as a response to so many clients who had many questions about the process of getting their books published. This slim volume lays out the step-by-step process to taking the big step of writing and publishing a book. With attention to detail and hard work, I know you will be successful. Good luck and let me know when you have achieved your dream!

John Bond

Acknowledgments

This book is an accumulation of knowledge that I have gained over the last thirty-plus years. I have learned so much from so many people. From the first author I spoke with about writing a textbook to discussing with other authors the sixth edition of their work, I have been the beneficiary of so much practical knowledge and hard-fought wisdom. I am at a loss at how to acknowledge so many people who taught me so much. Long-term connections with so many authors have become friendships. I have been privileged to be there with my book authors through marriages, births, new jobs, tenure, conferring of doctoral degrees, retirements, and books. Lots of books.

One other group of individuals I can acknowledge are the generous reviewers of the manuscript for this work in its present and previous forms. They all provided valuable, detailed suggestions. Any shortcomings in the book, however, are mine and do not reflect on them.

I would also like to acknowledge that this book draws on my previous books, including *The Little Guide to Getting Your Journal Article Published*, *The Little Guide to Giving Poster Presentations*, and most significantly *You Can Write and Publish a Book, Second Edition*.

Finally, I would like to acknowledge the ever-supportive Theresa Woolley. None of this is possible without you.

Introduction

How to Use This Book

The goal of this book is for you to learn how to turn your ideas into a published book. The content proceeds in a step-by-step fashion. Read the entire book once. Then go back and review the key parts, making your personalized plan with a timeline. Readers can cherry-pick chapters to focus on, but the value is understanding the process all the way through.

Some people write their whole book first and then seek a publisher or agent. Others develop a proposal and sample chapters and find a publisher or agent. They then write the whole manuscript. This book can be used for either path.

This book is geared toward nonfiction, including monographs, textbooks, and more academic works. The concepts apply whether you are interested in publishing a paper book, eBook, or both. This book is (mostly) discipline or subject-matter neutral. It is not a book just for STEM, the social sciences, or a specific subject area. Many of the concepts are universal. In some places, additional work on your part is needed to adapt these concepts to your particular subject matter or format.

In regard to language, I use book and manuscript interchangeably. There is a definite time when a manuscript becomes a book, but book is more pleasing to the ear. I have chosen to write this book in the familiar fashion ("when you are writing . . .") instead of the more academic form ("when one is writing . . ."). The book is meant to be a conversation between us.

I hope you enjoy it and find it useful.

John Bond

Part I

GETTING STARTED

Chapter 1

Starting with a Purpose

The secret of success is constancy to purpose. —Benjamin Disraeli

UNDERSTANDING YOUR GOALS

You have had a dream for some time. A need. Or maybe an urgency. Perhaps you are interested in putting your work forward in your community of experts or scholars. Or you feel your idea might find an audience with real sales potential. Maybe it will top its bestseller category at Amazon.

Where do you start? Begin by knowing your reasons for taking the journey. You will need to examine your motives. Sit down and make a list of why you want to write and publish a book. This list can be for your eyes only. List each reason in a few words. Make an actual list, as there will be multiple reasons on different levels for starting a project.

Be honest with yourself. Some of the reasons may be lofty (to advance the work being done in your field) while others may seem personal (for personal fulfillment or to make money). Whatever the reasons, write them all down.

Your list of reasons might be to:

- Publish the results of your work to gain the acceptance of your peers.
- Help people who do not understand the topic of your book.
- Demonstrate that you are an authority on the subject.

- Educate the next generation.
- Attain tenure.
- Advance in your career.
- Make money.
- Become famous.

This exercise will require you to look within and face your motives. Perhaps you have been motoring along feeling that writing a book is simply your destiny. This exercise might make you realize your true motivation. Honesty is the best policy here. Be true to yourself and your efforts. Once you are finished with your list, let it sit for a day or more and then come back to it. Look at it with a fresh set of eyes to see if it is complete. Likely there will be multiple reasons. Few people will have just one reason.

EVALUATING YOUR LIST

Take your list and evaluate its authenticity. Does it ring true about yourself and your ideas? Now put the reasons in order from the most important to the least important. The best way to do this is to ask yourself if you achieved only one of the goals, which would be the most satisfying? Then do this with each point on the remaining list until you have them all in order.

Think about the goals at the top of your list. Can they be achieved through other means? If you were looking to be recognized as an expert in a field, would being a speaker achieve the same results? If there are multiple paths to the same point, are your skills and interests best suited to achieve this goal by book publishing, or perhaps by an alternate route? You might achieve the same goal faster or more easily with alternate methods.

Look at the list and ask yourself if you achieved all of the goals except the first one, would you consider the project a success? Do any goals conflict with any others? What are the obstacles to achieving them? Time? Money? Expertise? Evaluate and plan how to address the obstacles.

While not required, it may be helpful to share your ideas with a colleague or close friend. If you decide to do this, pick someone you trust, and from whom you can accept frank observations. Not everyone will give you honest feedback, nor does everyone want it.

Ask their opinion of your potential project. Discuss your motivations. See if the person suggests additional ones that you did not include. They might suggest ones you did not list. Carefully consider the feedback. These comments may be difficult to accept if they contradict your perception of yourself.

Encouragement is important. If you choose to share the list, pick a positive, upbeat person, but one who is also honest. Publishing a book is an achievable goal if you are willing to spend the time and effort and have perseverance.

There is a lot of naysaying in the industry about your chances to publish your own work. Most of the people who say this are published authors, agents, or editors. You need to dream and to dream big. Expect the world, but also a challenging road ahead. However, if one of your goals is to be a *New York Times* bestselling author, and you do not make it, you will find that publishing a well-received, popular work is still a tremendous accomplishment.

Perhaps you will choose to self-publish. If so, the barriers to publishing are your own dedication, time, and money. Your work can spring to life based on your efforts, and you may find your ideal audience, at which point the mythical maze of finding a publisher or agent drops away.

The ultimate predictor of success will be your dedication. Tenacity, self-determination, and passion are the magic variables. These will be the factors that make your idea become a reality. At one time, your parents might have said, "you can do anything that you put your mind to." At one time it was true. But most of us eventually face reality. Some childhood dreams are likely now out of reach. Becoming an author, however, is one thing that it is never too late to do.

Start with a dream and an idea, assess your reasons for wanting to make it a reality, roll up your sleeves, resolve to finish the task, and make it happen.

Chapter 2

Understanding the Difference Between a Book, Textbook, and Monograph

The reading of all good books is like conversation with the finest minds of past centuries. —René Descartes

DEFINITIONS FIRST

This may seem like an unnecessary exercise but getting the terms right from the beginning is important. Here are some basic definitions:

- A textbook is a book containing a compilation of content in a branch of study to meet the needs of students and educators, usually at an educational institution.
- A monograph is a book for a specialist on a single subject or an aspect of a subject and usually on a scholarly topic. The primary purpose of a monograph is to present research and original scholarship. This research is presented at length, distinguishing a monograph from a journal article.
- A book is the broadest of the terms. A book is a format for presenting writing or images. The term book can be assumed to include both textbooks and monographs. Book (versus a monograph or textbook) more likely connotes a book found at a neighborhood bookstore such as a mass-market paperback or trade hardback.
- For clarity, eBooks are not a separate category. A monograph can be a paper book or in a digital version called an eBook, as can a textbook

or book. As of this date, eBooks by-and-large are not separate creations or formats (although certain companies and individuals might dispute this; and they might be right). Think of an eBook as a choice; the same way you might think of choosing between hardcover versus paperback. However, eBooks will emerge (sooner than expected) as something different than the paper book in digital form. They will become a hybrid somewhat more akin to websites and interactive learning modules, but the industry and market are not there yet.

• Likewise, audiobooks (and audio information in general) has exploded in recent years. Audiobooks are exactly that, the book being read aloud. They are, like eBooks, not a separate item but a format choice.

Of course, there is a gray zone between the terms book, monograph, and textbook. A monograph really is a book. A monograph can be used in a classroom and therefore it is also a textbook. A trade paperback from the top of a bestseller list can be used in the classroom. But classically, most people can spot a textbook by its interior presentation, or a monograph by its topic or authorship.

Through these chapters, the term book will be used primarily but remember that it is interchangeable in many instances for monograph or textbook. When there are specific discussions that require the more exact term (such as in a classroom), then the more precise term will be used.

One reminder, this book concerns itself with nonfiction. While many of the writing and publishing concepts apply to fiction or novels, the distinctive topics relating to getting a novel published are not addressed here.

GETTING EDUCATED

While defining terms, let us discuss the importance of education. Commit yourself at this point to becoming educated on writing, publishing, and marketing. Your personal knowledge will have a tremendously positive affect on the final product.

There are numerous books on writing and publishing. Some are listed in the bibliography at the end of this book. Read them. Become a student of the craft of writing. There are some great books on writing a book proposal, self-publishing, marketing your work, and many other areas. Dive in and start to absorb.

Joining local in-person or online writer groups can be very helpful. There are self-published author groups as well. LinkedIn has some great ones. Try them on and see which click with you.

There are also national groups that you can join for a modest fee, such as the Textbook & Academic Authors Association and the Independent Book Publishers Association. They give great guidance, and you will be around like-minded people.

Now, let us dig into your project.

Chapter 3

Defining Your Idea or Topic

To produce a mighty book, you must choose a mighty theme.
—Herman Melville

STARTING WITH YOU

To some of you, this chapter may seem unnecessary. You probably picked up this book because you have an exact idea in mind. Perhaps you have the structure or outline of the book already. You might even have a title.

Some of you may just want to be an author and have not yet determined what topic, or focus, suits you best. Maybe you love to write and are interested in a career change, possibly as a freelance writer or book author. You will need to commit to a topic, knowing that you can always adjust your subject as you develop the book.

To get started on choosing a topic, make a list—all about you. Focus on your fields of study or areas of expertise. Make a list of the jobs you have had including any side interests or hobbies. Your list should not just be a mini-résumé of your life but a descriptive and subjective look at your strengths. Keep making lists. Have blue-sky sessions with yourself or your friends and family. After you have your list of everything connected to you, it is time to synthesize it. Use a combination of what you are best at and what you are most passionate about to prioritize it.

Part of the equation for you may be understanding what genres or types of books sell and what do not. This may matter to you, or this may not be part of your motivation for writing. Research becomes essential in understanding the marketability of a topic.

To find out which topics have many books, and which have few, try looking in your local bookstore or at an online bookseller. Books on programming are much more popular than home computer repair. Textbooks outsell monographs.

Do all these points seem obvious to you? Good, that means you are already thinking about what people want. If you do research on your topic and find few books in your area, that is not necessarily bad or good news. What matters most is your approach to the topic, and your ability to define an audience. Future chapters will discuss defining your idea and your market. Pick a topic for your book. Do not be afraid to make a choice. It is early in the publishing process. You can always start over.

Now to proceed; commit to an exact idea for your book.

Chapter 4

Developing a Title and Summary

If any man wish to write in a clear style, let him be first clear in his thoughts. —Johann Wolfgang von Goethe

COMMITTING, FOR NOW

You have a defined idea. Now it is time to come up with a title and summarize your book in a few sentences. Many people's reaction will be that it is too early in the process. Take a breath. This may sound like an important task, and one that you might feel is misplaced in your timeline. It is, however, a key step. Realize that while it should be done now, it is not set in stone. These exercises help you focus what your book covers but also, most importantly, what your book does *not* cover.

Creating a title and summary this early in the process will help you focus on the right direction. Many people are unhappy about the current state of society insisting that everything can be defined in a few words. Many topics, people will claim, are so complex that they cannot be boiled down that way. While this may be true in some instances, it should not be the case for most nonfiction books. People will need to quickly grasp what your work entails.

When the book is first published, and you are asked by an acquaintance or stranger what your book is about, you may go to great lengths to describe it. Some people will not want that level of detail and will tune you out. As time goes by, you will start to reflexively pare the description down. You will learn what parts of the description are essential and help them to quickly understand your book.

THE ALL-IMPORTANT TITLE

The title is more important than almost anything having to do with your book (only rivaled by the cover). Accept this fact. Treat the title with the respect and the importance it deserves.

If you are going to spend too much time on any of the tasks, this is the one. The differences between a good and great title are quickly apparent. And if you are fortunate enough to think up a great title, you will know it instantly when you see it on the faces of the people who hear it.

To get started requires some introspection. What is the heart of your book? What is the most important part to you? To your reader? What are the secondary topics that, while important, will not be immediately evident in the title? For example, while this book covers writing a title for a book, it is not immediately obvious that it is discussed here, judging by this book's title.

Take the time necessary to think about what you really want to write. Think about what you want to focus on. You will undoubtedly come to a crossroads and will need to make some important decisions.

The task of creating a title, however, is not final. Write one as if it were permanent, but be aware that it may, and is likely to, be revised or tweaked as the book becomes a reality.

Start out by making a list of key words or phrases that cover the subject of your book. Think of synonyms or common phrases associated with the topic. Be willing to think outside the box. After you have made your list of key words and possible phrases, start to play with their order. Be open to different perspectives and do not become married to the first one you like. Be willing to start from scratch.

It is helpful to make a list of common expressions, clichés, and quotations that might work with your topic or title. Be open-minded and cast a wide net. Think about words associated with the work. Be careful, however, of going too far and being too cute or trite.

Most nonfiction books will have a title and subtitle. They will be separated by a colon. The title will be the most important part. The subtitle will come after the colon and help to clarify the topic of the book.

The subtitle can be longer than the title. An important note is that the title should explain the book completely by itself because sometimes they may not appear together. Some directories, websites, and booksellers only list the title and not the subtitle. Test-drive just the title with a few friends to see their reactions. See if they can determine the topic of the book.

It may help to browse through the aisles of a brick-and-mortar bookstore. How do other people browse in the store as well, and which books are picked up? Stay away from the books in your topic area. Be original. You will gain more from examples of books on other topics.

Come up with a list of five or more titles that you think work. Some words or phrases may be common from title to title. Rank your draft titles in the order you prefer.

Now you will need some outside opinions. Start with a group of trusted friends or acquaintances and share the list. Ask them which ones they like and which they do not like and why. Ask them what they think the book is about. Make notes on everything and be open to all ideas.

As you use this feedback to refine your ideas, you should narrow down your possible titles to two or three. Keep asking people, but make sure the group is diverse in knowledge. Ask people at school, at work, or wherever you meet them. If you have a small group that is available to you, hold a mini-focus group. Keep refining until you have a title that works for you. If a title constantly gets negative feedback, let it go. You may love it, but if the book sits untouched on the store shelves, that would be worse.

One final step is the search engine test. Think about how easily your title can be spelled. How can the words be confused or juxtaposed? If someone puts the key words into a search engine incorrectly, what would the results be? Go to an online bookseller and put the title into the "Advanced Search" option. What comes up? What if words are left out or transposed? Misspelled? Avoid words that are difficult to spell.

Of course, some textbooks and monographs will have extremely technical or specialized words in the title. Phacoemulsification is a complex and difficult word to spell, let alone pronounce, but if you are an ophthalmologist interested in a book on this topic, it is all too common and simple to spell.

Remember, when you settle on a title, it can still change. However, for the time being, consider it final.

Here are some pieces of advice for helping you create your ideal title. For every piece of advice or rule, there are exceptions:

- The shorter the better.
- It should be easy to remember. Tell it to a couple of people and see if they remember it a few minutes later. Check with some of them the next day to see if they remember it.
- Do not become attached to any one title, or part of a title. Be open to all ideas.
- Think of the title as a tool for marketing and sales as much as a descriptor of your content.
- Try to make the title positive. Unless it is a book on a controversial topic, people want to feel there are positive (or at least not negative) answers to problems. There are exceptions.
- Try to avoid a title that is overly cute, or one that uses a very trendy word. Titles that capitalize on trendy terms may date the book too quickly. Exceptions are if the book is focusing on that trend.
- Avoid dates or words that date a book to a period of time, unless that is the focus of the work.
- When you have your final title, say it aloud many times to see how it sounds, and how easy it is to say.
- As a final task, compare your title to other books in this area to make sure you have not consciously or unconsciously created one that mirrors a rival book (Bond, 2018).

For the title, thinking about keywords is important. Keywords are terms used to connect items like your book to other items such as websites, books, and a host of other content. Think through the keywords that would associate your book with what your audience might be searching.

CREATING YOUR SUMMARY

Now you will need to summarize your whole book in three short takes. Come up with a one-sentence description, a one-paragraph description, and a three-paragraph description of the book. This is a deceptively challenging assignment.

How would you want an interviewer to complete the sentence, "And tomorrow on the podcast is an author who wrote a book that . . ." The interviewer will need to tell the viewers quickly and they will need to precisely convey your topic.

What would you have someone say if they were going to run an excerpt of your book on a website and offered to start out with a one-paragraph (four to five short sentences) description of the book? How would you describe your work?

Finally, a friend of yours said they will hand out a flier to their book club about your project. The book club members are the ideal readers for your topic. You can use up to three paragraphs to describe the book. What would you say to these potential buyers?

As you write your future book proposal, and then your book, all of these items can change. They will be useful in the marketing description, in your listing at online booksellers, and with promotional efforts by your publishers. Again, these exercises are meant to help you focus on what you really want to say and what your book is about and what is not covered in your work.

The best way to come up with these three levels of descriptions is to create a rough table of contents. The number of chapters is not important at this stage, just getting the logical sequence down will help. The chapter titles can be just a few words to describe the topics—no need to worry about polished, final chapter titles. You might list twenty chapters and the final book could have ten or thirty. This simply helps you get down what is, and what is not, going to be covered.

Take the table of contents and translate it into the three-paragraph description. Remember, the first sentence and first paragraph are the most important. If the reader does not get past the first sentence, they will never get to the rest of the description. When writing this description, think about what question people will want answered about the book. Will your book be a simple guide or a definitive work? Will it be full of photos and illustrations or just text? Will it be written for the novice or expert?

Think about these items as you focus on describing (and thereby, preparing to write) your book. This early focus will pay dividends and ease your task later.

To help you decide what your book is about, think about competitive books. Many prospective authors say, "there is no book like mine," but there is always at least one book (and most likely several) that people could buy *instead* of yours. Or they could buy nothing!

When you have a rough draft of the three paragraphs, move on to boiling them down to the one-paragraph description. Do not just take the first paragraph. Then you can move on to the all-important single sentence. Every word is precious and essential. Make sure one sentence is one sentence and not a run-on, jam-packed sentence (Bond, 2018).

As you progress, you may need to go back and revise what you just created. Taking your time with each step will force you to reevaluate what gets said and what gets left out. Take your time.

Think about the format of your book. Workbooks, books that fit in your pocket, and coffee table books are just a few of the options. Think about which one is best suited to your material.

Understanding your potential readers and their buying habits is very helpful. To understand this, a key question to consider is how people buy books. If you are browsing in the gardening or cookbook sections and you are not searching for a specific book, how would you decide which one to buy? It is probably an intricate combination of cover design, title, price, size/appearance, familiarity with the topic and author, endorsements on the covers, and your mood.

As an exercise, go into a large bookstore and browse for a cookbook on Mediterranean cuisine or a self-help book. See where you are drawn and what attracts you. You may also ask a friend to do this exercise for you and have them speak aloud what comes to mind when choosing a book.

It cannot be emphasized enough how important it is to spend time in bookstores and libraries and get to know the people who work there. Many independent (and chain) bookstore managers and employees know their customers and books very well. If they walk up to the history section, they can probably point to the ones that sell (and therefore the ones that do not). They may not always know what people love about the book, but they certainly know which ones are most popular.

Also, when you are in the bookstore or online, note the section where your book would be shelved. Compare it to the other sections of the bookstore in size. Are the books shelved by the author's last name or by subcategory (as in history)? Ask the bookseller what is selling well in the store. What is the biggest surprise seller?

Remember this may not be applicable if a bookstore will not be the primary place your book is purchased. It would be ideal if there was a monograph or textbook store, but there is not (or at least not in the way there are large chain bookstores). Even if there is not a physical place to browse for your intended book, this exercise can still help you better understand your customers and how they choose one title over another. Up to now, you have summarized your topic in a few sentences. You have an emerging vision of your book. Looking forward, you will need to start to think about where to take your book idea and how to present it.

Chapter 5

Defining Your Ideal Reader or Customer

If you would be a reader, read; if a writer, write. —Epictetus

WHO ARE THEY?

Another piece of the puzzle as you prepare to write your book and find a publisher is understanding who your audience is. This may seem obvious to some people. "The audience is students taking a particular class." Or "People who are a certain profession." If you have such a defined group, this is great. Others might stumble and say, "I have a very broad audience. Everyone can benefit from my work!" Or "I am not sure who the audience is; I just know it will be very popular." Or "I will leave that up to the publisher."

Defining your ideal reader (and therefore your market) now will help focus your work, help secure a publisher, and eventually help you sell more books.

An ideal reader is a concept that writers use to focus their work. Many times, writers will envision an exact person they know when writing to help make the innumerable decisions they face. Do you assume your reader has a certain level of knowledge? Are they a novice or well-versed? What level of education do they have? Imagining an ideal reader is a helpful first step in understanding your audience.

The next step is thinking about how to find them. For textbooks, it is not where to find the students but where to find the educators or instructors who would consider the use of the book in a class. For monographs, where does this specialized audience "congregate"? They probably do not literally gather, but where do they learn and share ideas?

As an example, maybe you are writing a monograph about the use of artificial intelligence in the creation of new pharmaceuticals. Who will be interested in this book? Likely audiences are scientists, computer programmers, medical professionals, business executives, marketers, entrepreneurs. But where would a publisher connect with them? Which conferences or conventions would they attend? Which professional or trade associations are they members of? What news sites do they read? Which social media channels do they frequent? These points, and many like them, help ground the audience in an exact place.

As you proceed with writing your book, keep notes on the audience. This will help with the proposal later, as well as the promotion of your work. Keep notes on the highest level (e.g., the audience is nurses), a more grounded level (e.g., specifically, they are geriatric and hospice nurses interested in end-of-life care), and granular details (e.g., they attend Gerontological Society of America's annual meeting). Refine your notes as you proceed.

When you come to a fork in the road with content creation ("Should I include this chapter?" "Should I cover this topic in depth?"), refer to these notes to guide you. Let your ideal reader or audience/customer profile educate your decisions.

Chapter 6

Deciding on Sole or Coauthorship

If you want to go fast, go alone; if you want to go far, go together.
—Anonymous

THE DIFFERENCES BETWEEN AUTHOR AND EDITOR

Some people using this book will want to write work by themselves. Others will have valued coauthors or coeditors for their project. Others will ask colleagues to contribute chapters. The decision to go it alone or with a coauthor is not one to make too quickly.

First, when someone is called an author, it usually means they write the entire work themselves. Sometimes an author includes a section or chapter contributed by another. On the other hand, an editor is someone who brings together many contributors. The editor envisions the work, asks colleagues or experts to write on specific topics, and then ensures all of the contributions work together in content and in form. An editor may still write chapters or portions of the book.

The pros and cons of each circumstance are easy to enumerate. Solo authors have a whole book to write but they make all the decisions themselves. There is no waiting on contributors that never submit nor trying to rewrite chapters to fit the tone of the book. Bottom line: being the sole author takes a lot of time but there are no control issues. Having coauthors (that is, writing is split between two or so people) is similar to solo authorship. If you have a good rapport with the coauthor and know each other's

23

work habits, it can be a fine arrangement. Having said that, things happen. Life can intervene and deadlines get missed or quality can slip. There is more control, but you are still dependent on someone else.

If you are considering coauthoring with someone that you do not have a long connection with, take it slow. Go into any such arrangement with your eyes wide open. Be clear over the division of responsibilities. Who writes what, who edits what, who reviews what, etc. should all be agreed on ahead of time. Have these understandings all written down, including the order of authorship on the cover. Do not "leave it for later" to be decided. As for your part, under-promise and over-deliver regarding deadlines. Honesty is the best policy when it comes down to this relationship. Consider having an "out clause" in case someone has a life event that means they need to withdraw from the project. Understand who will "own" the material that may have already been created and who can use it in the future. Share these details with your publisher when that time comes.

As for being an editor, there is less time that you will spend writing and more time on organization and follow-up. Likely you will reach out to a group of experts asking them to write a chapter or section of the book. You would provide them details such as word count, deadline, figure/table count, and format. You might also provide a sample chapter to show tone and approach.

After getting people to sign on, you will then spend time answering questions, chasing them down, and (potentially) refining their submissions. You will deal with a contributor or two who just goes silent or does not deliver. If you have asked twenty people to contribute, likely one or two will let you down. Plan on it and have a backup for either someone else or yourself to step in.

As for pros as an editor, there is considerably less writing for you to do but more coordination and follow-up. There is lack of control of course. If you choose to have a coeditor, the time is further reduced for you, but also more elements are introduced outside your control.

CONSIDERING YOUR NETWORK

A factor to consider when choosing between being an author or an editor is how wide and deep your network is. If you have lots of people to call on to contribute, bravo. Conversely, if you are unsure who to ask or how to find people to write, this could be a concern. However, do not despair if you do not have a deep contact list. You can always go to the people you know to find or ask the people *they* know. Six degrees of separation has now become half as close—maybe only three degrees. If you do invite someone recommended by a contact, research them. Try to ensure they are a good fit from various standpoints including their content knowledge, subject-philosophical perspective, reliability, and temperament. If they are not a good match, save yourself the headaches and do not invite them.

At the end of the day, deciding on writing the book yourself, with a partner, or as an editor is an intricate decision, based on your schedule and interest in control. Take your time to make the best decision for you.

You have envisioned your project and created a tentative title and description. You understand your market and who your audience is. You have made the decision on authorship Enjoy your progress. Now it is time to develop a plan, a timeline, and get moving.

Part II

WRITING YOUR MANUSCRIPT

Chapter 7

Developing a Plan

How do you eat an elephant? One bite at a time. —Anonymous

UNDERSTANDING THE STEPS IN PUBLISHING

You have built your foundation. Now it is time to get down to work. The next two chapters will help you develop a plan and create a timeline for writing and getting your book published.

There is no set path for the work ahead. You have two tasks: write the book and find a publisher or agent. You can do all the writing and then find a publisher or agent. Or you can create a full book proposal, query letter, and find an agent or publisher. Then you would write the book. The most likely scenario is that you will interweave these tasks together. As an aside, self-publishing will be addressed as a separate path.

Whichever direction you choose, create a customized plan. The generic steps in book publishing are:

- Develop an idea, title, and brief description.
- Decide on being an author or editor.
- Create a draft table of contents.
- Draft each chapter in outline form.
- Complete the literature review and or research.
- Accumulate your information.

- Acquire any images, graphics, or tables.
- Start drafting each chapter.
- Complete the first draft of the whole manuscript.
- Do one complete edit.
- Try to find colleagues, friends, or peer reviewers to read the draft.
- Continue editing. Run grammar checks.
- Submit to reviewers.
- Get comments back and make final edits.
- Create a dynamic book proposal and query letter.
- Carefully research publishers or agents. Submit your material.
- Secure a publisher. Review and sign their publishing agreement.
- Submit the manuscript in its proper form.
- Receive page proofs and cover design and review them closely.
- All the while, be creating your Author Promotional Platform.
- Do prelaunch book promotion and publicity.
- Your book publishes!
- Continue to market and promote your book.
- Start your second book.

Each step contains many, many sub-steps. The tasks are intertwined and there is no set order. As a future book author, you will juggle many balls in the air.

Break each step down into smaller steps. As an example, one task might be to do a literature review. Instead of simply listing "literature review" as a step in your customized plan, you may wish to indicate steps, such as: visit the library (in person or remote), set a meeting with a librarian, search databases, download articles, read articles, and analyze articles. A longer list looks more daunting than a shorter one but crossing steps off it each day will undoubtedly be gratifying and give you a sense of accomplishment.

Develop a Task List

Start to develop your task list and add to it as you proceed through this book. The list should be updated through the whole writing and publishing process. At the end of this book is a sample Publication Plan.

It will also be helpful to keep a running to-do list. It will serve as a reminder to do the innumerable small- and medium-sized tasks ahead.

As an aside, establishing an amenable workspace can also be important. Some people can read or write anywhere and not be distracted. This is not true for everyone. Try to establish a simple workplace with reduced or minimal distractions. For some, this may sound far-fetched, but even relocating to the library may provide a better environment. Distraction-free writing and editing is key; or it can be. The great writer Toni Morrison told her students, "One of the most important things they need to know is when they are their best, creatively. They need to ask themselves: What does the ideal room look like? Is there music or silence? Is there chaos outside or is there serenity outside? What do I need in order to release my imagination?"

Developing a plan and the accompanying timeline is one of the most concrete steps you can take to stay on track for writing and publishing your book. Only by seeing that the process is composed of individual tasks can you conquer any concerns you have about your ability to achieve your goal.

Studiously work the plan! You will be pleased you did.

Chapter 8

Developing a Timeline

A journey of a thousand miles begins with a single step. —*Lao Tzu*

ADVICE FROM VETERAN AUTHORS

Equally important to the personalized Publication Plan is the creation of a realistic timeline. For each step in the plan, assign dates for completion. Consider assigning an exact time of day and the length of time for each task.

A few pieces of advice from veteran authors regarding the development of a timeline:

- It needs to be realistic. Being overly optimistic or pessimistic does not serve you well.
- You should have a firm end date for submission and potentially for publication.
- When assigning dates, try to work on the book most days. Completing a little bit of the project each day will give you a (justified) sense of accomplishment.
- Keep yourself accountable to the schedule you create. Of course, bumps in the road will occur, and you may miss a date, but a commitment is a commitment. You must whittle away at the project each week if you are going to get your work published. Creating regular

work habits is a key to ongoing writing and publishing success. Set
times and stick to them.

- When creating a schedule, incremental steps are more valuable than
  big blocks of time, which are likely to be borrowed from when other
  tasks in your life demand your attention. Do not just block out time
  on your calendar to "write." Other theories suggest that finding large
  blocks of quiet time is best. Do what works for you.
- There are some great apps that can help you keep track of your tasks
  and schedule. They will graphically show your progress and remind
  you of your commitments. Some are likely available through your
  smartphone or laptop. Alternatively, search productivity apps for the
  best ones (Bond, 2018).

As you start to work on your plan, you may find many reasons why you
are not meeting your time commitments. Keeping to a writing schedule
is one of the most difficult parts of the process, particularly for people
with hectic lives.

TYPICAL REASONS FOR NOT WRITING

Here are some of the most common reasons that people do *not* stick to
their writing schedule, followed by the reasons *not* to buy into them:

- *You are busy at work.* Protect your writing time in your schedule.
  Of course, your duties at work are important. But so is writing and
  publishing. In the big picture, writing and publishing have a more
  significant impact on your career than any day-to-day responsibilities. Writing needs to be treated as the all-important activity it is.
- *You are busy at home.* This goes without saying, but it is important to
  segment your writing from the workplace and home. Try to consider
  finding time at home as possible opportunities to write. Whether it is
  watching TV or scrolling through social media, there is likely time to
  redirect toward your writing and publishing.
- *You are not a good writer.* Almost all writers and academics doubt
  their writing ability. The best advice anyone can give is that the more
  you write, the more you will improve as a writer. Whether it is journal-
  aling on a personal basis or writing a report for work, all will improve

your overall writing ability. Read widely in your area of interest and outside your field. Becoming a dedicated reader will make you a better writer and a more accomplished person.

- *There is more research to do.* While this may be true, at some point, the researching and literature review phase must conclude. Some authors use an open-ended literature review as an excuse to not commence on the rest of the project. It is not to suggest you perform a mediocre literature review. But instead set a definitive time and concentrate all your energies during that time.
- *Major developments are happening in your field.* Your book is a moment in time. It is unlikely the final word in any area as almost all topics are evolving. Carefully consider if these developments are truly going to change your field or are you just using this as an excuse not to move forward.
- *Your work has been rejected in the past.* If you spoke with successful authors, you would find out that almost all of them have received rejections, some of them had more than their share. Accept rejection as part of the process and not a personal commentary on you or your work.
- *Procrastination.* We are all subject to putting things off. It is a human condition. You must ask yourself these questions: Do you want to be published? Do you want to advance in your field? Do you want your ideas and work to become part of the intellectual discourse? If yes, then you need to find the intestinal fortitude to overcome procrastination and become dedicated to the process of writing and publishing (Bond, 2018).

Do not let these reasons sidetrack you or worse. Think positive, develop a plan, and assign timelines to every step.

Developing a plan and setting a timeline comprise the most important steps in writing and publishing a book. Tightly defining your idea and setting out a detailed plan lays out the foundation for everything else that will follow in the book and can help ensure your success. Do not proceed with the rest of the book until you have embraced these key steps.

Chapter 9

Understanding the Parts of a Book

It does not matter how slowly you go as long as you do not stop.
—Confucius

WHAT IS WHAT

You are almost ready to really dig in, but there's one last step before putting fingertips to keyboard. Let us define some terms for the various parts of a book:

- *Sections/Chapters*: You will probably separate your book into chapters. There may be larger themes that you would like to group your chapters into. Review the sections in this book to see how the groupings help the reader understand the major themes in your work. As a general rule of thumb, shorter sentences and shorter paragraphs are better than longer, denser ones. There are exceptions but the market has moved toward shorter, more focused works than massive, voluminous ones. Few readers ever said, "I wish that book was longer."
- *Illustrations*: Your book may have photographs or drawings. They can be essential to your material. They can also become very expensive unless you are able to provide them yourself. You will need to discuss with the publisher who will be responsible for creating them. Also, in print books, the majority of photographs or illustrations in the book should be in black and white. Color, other than on the cover,

is very expensive (of course this does not apply to eBooks). Exceptions are coffee-table books, cookbooks, children's picture books, and some technical works. Finally, the photographs or illustrations are one of many factors that will influence readers to buy (or not to buy) your book. If you are going to have photographs or illustrations, make sure they are high quality. More later on creating and choosing images in chapter 12.

- *Third-Party Content*: You may choose to use material from other sources. If you want to use a significant portion, you will need to seek permission from the original source. Respect the copyrights of others and when in doubt, seek permission to use the material. If you are using any third-party content and are unsure if it is permissible, consult with your publisher. Be prepared—there is likely a fee. If you do ask for permission from the source, make sure you ask for permission for nonexclusive rights, worldwide, for all formats. Also, acknowledge all materials that are from other sources with a credit line showing the source.

The material that runs before the first chapter is known as the front matter, and the material that runs after the last chapter is the back matter, sometimes called end matter. The publisher (which might be you if you are self-publishing) will be responsible for knowing what goes on some of these pages, such as the copyright page and title pages. Here is a brief explanation of the various parts. First the front matter:

- *Testimonials Page*: Starts off the book and will list the endorsements or testimonials you have received. It is more marketing than part of the content of the book.
- *Title Page*: Lists your title, the publisher, place of publication, and your name. If you have an advanced degree, you should list this here. Also, if it is a technical book, you may want to list your affiliation or place of employment to establish your credibility.
- *Copyright Page*: Lists the standard copyright disclaimer, contact information for the publisher, cataloging information, and Library of Congress data. This is the publisher's responsibility.
- *Dedication*: Your chance to dedicate the work to someone.
- *Table of Contents*: A listing of the chapter titles and other sections or parts of the book, with appropriate page numbers.

- *Acknowledgments*: Your chance to acknowledge the people who helped you with the book. It is okay to list people you have not met but who may have influenced you. Send them a copy of the book. Maybe they will endorse it. Also, do not forget your parents.
- *List of Photographs/Maps/Charts/Illustrations*: Create a list of these items that allows the reader to easily find them in the book.
- *Foreword*: Usually written by someone else, preferably someone famous or influential in your chosen field. It should be an endorsement of you and your book.
- *Preface*: Written by you, it tells why you wrote the book or what inspired you to create it. Use it to establish your credentials.
- *Introduction*: Written by you, it usually tells for whom you wrote the book. The introduction also should include the information a reader would need to know about how the book is set up, or any special instructions on how to read or use it.
- For the foreword, preface, and the introduction, keep them short. They are not likely to be read, and it is better to put the good stuff in the book.

Here are the parts of the back matter:

- *Bibliography or References*: This is the list of materials you used to create your book. There are rules about how to list them. Books such as the *Chicago Manual of Style* can help you cite each item correctly.
- *Appendix*: The appendix is additional materials or documents the reader may find valuable. Think of these resources as bonuses.
- *Glossary*: The glossary is a short listing of technical terms dealing with the topic of the book. It includes a definition for each term.
- *Index*: With a print book, a listing of terms from the book with the associated page number comprises the index. Make sure the index is a significant length. It is a valuable tool for the reader and some people will use it to decide whether to buy the book or not. It reflects on the quality of the book. Many eBooks do not have an index but utilize the search function instead.
- *About the Author*: Do not be humble. Make sure you list any other publications you have, as well as anything that qualifies you to write the book. It can run in the front matter or back matter (Bond, 2018).

Now, let us start to talk about writing your book and then getting it published.

Chapter 10

Creating Chapter Outlines

Words are all we have. —Samuel Beckett

CREATING THE FRAMEWORK

You have a plan and a timeline. Now you have to actually get started on writing the book. A whole book. How do you take the leap?

A reminder: there is no set path for the work ahead. You have to write the book and find a publisher or agent. You can do all the writing and then find a publisher or agent. Or you can create a full book proposal and query letter and find an agent or publisher. Then you would write the book. The most likely scenario is that you will interweave these tasks together. Let us assume you are going to create the book first before finding a publisher.

In chapter 4, you created a brief description as well as a draft table of contents. This is your jumping-off point. You will need to gradually expand each chapter title until you end up with the completed book. Start by taking each chapter title and placing it at the top of a page. Do not worry about how the exact chapter structure might be split into two or merge with another. This is simply a way to start to organize your material.

Add to each chapter a list of broad points that detail the concepts to be discussed. They will probably flow in a logical, sequential order. Some may just be miscellaneous items to be covered in that chapter.

Continue to do this for each chapter. When you are done, you will essentially have a list of all the topics you will cover in your book.

Through the process being discussed in this chapter, be open to changing your thinking. This step of adding broad topics to each of your chapters may uncover that some of them are packed while others are sparse. This may lead you to split or combine chapters. Now is the time to do this. Do not wait. Be open to the changes. This step is as much a discovery and educational process for you as it is a writing task.

These broad points or topics may eventually become the headings in your chapters. The headings do not need to be polished; they simply explain what will be covered in the chapter. Once you have this structure, you can start to add other subtopics to the page. Keep adding until you start to exceed a page on each chapter. Then keep expanding the list of items and points. When you start to feel it is becoming a dense, comprehensive list, it is time to write.

This method of getting started works. However, after you create the extended outline, you might get the feeling that this is a huge task. Well, to be honest, it is a time-consuming journey but not an insurmountable one.

Chapter 11

Writing Your First Draft

Whether you think you can or think you can't, you're right.
—Henry Ford

GETTING STARTED

You have an extended outline. Now it is time to sit down and write. No one said this would be easy or quick. You have your book description and table of contents. This will be your jumping-off point.

You will need to gradually expand each outline into a full draft of a chapter. You might want to consider starting with a middle chapter; one that is more run-of-the-mill. The first chapter can sometimes be intimidating. Wherever you start, give it your best try. It may be slow at first as you find your voice.

You might also be working out the mechanics of the project. Will you be writing in the third person or first person? Working out active voice versus passive voice takes time. Have you used gender-neutral language? What is your normal sentence and paragraph length? Do not be discouraged as you set the stage with your first chapter. This ground-work will make the rest of the writing easier. Completing one chapter will give you a sense of accomplishment.

Create a schedule for writing. Set aside time each day to whittle away at your project. Leave occasional days off to give yourself a breather. You should also set manageable amounts to be accomplished each day.

Be realistic and do not set expectations so high that you will become discouraged if you fall behind.

Write the entire book before you do any significant editing or revising. Completing the whole first draft will give you a tremendous sense of accomplishment. If, however, you find yourself at a crossroads with a topic or chapter that you have written, it is better to deal with the content decisions at that time rather than discarding or reworking the whole book later.

The length of time it will take to write your manuscript will vary greatly. Factors affecting this include the size of the book you are writing, research to be done, your comfort with writing and revising, your schedule, tasks competing for your time, and your perfectionism quotient.

One other concept to consider when approaching your writing is storytelling. This is not an idea most writers or readers associate with nonfiction books.

Your goal is to write your book. You want to make a difference. Part of the way to make this happen is by having readers consume the entire book. Using storytelling (even in textbooks or monographs) is one way to ensure you genuinely engage with the reader.

Humans love stories, and factual writing is no exception. Traditionally, stories involve setup, tension, action, climax, with eventual resolution. Think about your work using this concept. Take the reader on a journey by building a compelling story (or narrative).

WHAT SOFTWARE WORKS BEST?

As you embark on writing your book, you might want to consider what software you are using. Microsoft Word and Apple Pages are fine programs that can get the job done. Using other writing software programs has become popular. Programs such as Evernote, Grammarly, and others have gained popularity. Many of these programs offer dedicated writing tools and have integrated bibliographic management aspects.

In regard to the writing part (as opposed to managing your references), most basic writing software, such as Word, suffices. You will still need to do the writing and go through several rounds of editing. For writing, keep it simple with basic writing software. If you want additional help with the references and managing your bibliography, then consider programs dedicated to this function.

An idea to consider if you are feeling bogged down with the physical act of writing the book is to dictate the text. There are several options. Before you seek an outside solution, look toward your laptop and smartphone. All of the major operating systems and word processing systems come with built-in dictation software. The ones to consider are Microsoft Word Speech to Text, Apple Dictation, and Google Docs Voice Typing.

These features have limitations, in which case you might wish to turn to outside software. By far the longest serving and most sophisticated is Dragon or DragonSpeak. It has been around for more than twenty years and has developed an admirable suite of products. Others to consider include Otter.ai, Dictation.io, and Speechnotes.

Dictation software works best when you have composed your thoughts, considering what you will say, as opposed to free-form composition. When you are "making it up as you go along," it can come off as rambling and require significant editing (Bond, 2022b).

Technical language and dictation was a hurdle in the past. No longer—as the industry has adapted to the medical field, all other areas have benefited with specific vocabulary it recognizes or that you can add. Likewise, non-English language words were an issue. This has been addressed as most of these products offer versions in many languages.

Years ago, there were a lot more keyboard commands and vocal commands to know. The whole industry has gotten a lot more intuitive and easier to use. When you get started, it is best to invest some time and understand the way the software works. "New line," "new paragraph," "scratch that," and more may come naturally but there are so many other editing and formatting options. A bit of patience at the beginning will increase your output and efficiency. If you are skeptical, start small with your laptop software. Play around with it. It can be a good productivity tool.

No matter how you create your first pass of your book, keep all drafts of all your work. Name the documents in a way you will understand, such as Draft 1.0, Draft 2.0, etc. If you have a document of just your research or references, name it as such and keep everything. There is no reason to delete the old drafts or write over them. You never know when you may need your past work.

Do not keep all your work on your local hard drive. Learn to work off the cloud, or at least save to the cloud. File hosting services are prevalent and inexpensive. Services such as Google Drive, Microsoft OneDrive, Dropbox, or many others will ensure you never lose your work. Ruthlessly organize and back up everything you do!

Chapter 12

Adding Tables and Figures

It is like icing on the cake. —Anonymous

ADDING VISUALS FOR THE READERS

Let us take a break from your first draft before you move on to editing. Non-text items, such as figures and tables, are essential to textbooks and many other genres of books. They draw readers into your work and help illustrate the concepts being discussed. They might be a table of statistics, a graphic to illustrate a process, or maybe a historical photo. No matter what they are, readers want them, and they are more likely to make a book sell and be read.

First, a figure is a graphical representation of a concept. Figures can come in the form of several different categories:

- Photographs.
- Line drawings or line art.
- Charts and graphs. This last group can be further broken down into bar charts, flow charts, pie charts, line charts, histograms, and many others.

All these items go under the category of figures.

A table is a method of presenting data involving rows and columns of information. Tables can present data or help the reader analyze the results. Tables, as with figures, can come in various formats, including simple tables and multidimensional tables.

Here are a few suggestions when creating figures and tables for your book:

• *Use only original material.* Avoid using tables or figures from other sources. Doing this complicates the process and requesting permission to reuse content from other sources can slow down your efforts. Plus, it can be expensive.
• *Keep it simple.* Do not overdesign these items. Readers want to be able to get to the heart of what is being discussed.
• *Do not repeat information.* Tables and figures should be where you present the data. Do not repeat the data from the text in a table or vice versa.
• *Use dedicated programs to create them.* There are several programs specifically designed to create high-quality charts and tables. Microsoft Word and Excel can present data in a pleasing manner but there are also more sophisticated programs, such as Adobe Illustrator, Canva, MATLAB, SigmaPlot, and others.
• *Be mindful of color usage.* A reminder—some readers are color vision deficient. You can create graphics using shading or dots and dashes that allow anyone to understand the data (Bond, 2023a).

Each figure and table needs to be cited in the book's text, such as Table 1, Table 2, Figure 1, Figure 2. Figures and tables are numbered separately. Tables have headings, and figures have captions. Do not assume the reader will see the text that references the item. For other formatting decisions, such as capitalizing words in the table title and more, see the style manual in your field or the guidelines from your publisher. Some publishers might ask you to specify the size of the figure, often in terms of width (e.g., page width, column width or half-page width, two-thirds page width, etc.).

As an aside, some books have started including videos with accompanying websites (more on this to come). Talk to your publisher to see if such a website with videos is a possibility. Videos can be powerful tools to illustrate a point, such as a procedure or experiment.

Chapter 13

Keeping Track of Sources and References

If I have seen further (than others), it is by standing on the shoulders of giants. —Isaac Newton

CITE, CITE, CITE

You may have started your project with a literature search. In fact, the years prior to thinking about writing a book may have been one long quest for knowledge that underpins all of your writing and work. When you are ready to get down to writing your book, now is the time to formalize your quest for sources.

Research using the library or internet is a key step as well. You will need to research and verify what information and data go into your project. Once a reader starts to find statements that they know are not true, they will start to question everything else as well. Spend the time, do the legwork, and get the research done, and do it right the first time. Keep notes on all the facts that you derive from your research, so you know where the information came from. Cite your sources and never ever use material that is not your own.

References are essential to your final product. They should support your work and your conclusions. References follow a specific format by discipline or by publisher. Consult the style manual in your field or your publisher's guidelines.

There is a fine line between too few and too many references. Include the classic ones in your field and the ones that directly support your work. Do not turn your reference section into a bibliography of all the work published on the topic. On the other hand, to avoid plagiarism, any statement you make that ultimately comes from another source should include a citation in the text and a corresponding reference. A good practice while you are writing is to add a placeholder entry in the references (e.g., "Smith, 2023") every time you cite a new source in your text.

Astute readers of scholarly works or monographs may peruse the references in your book to evaluate its thoroughness. They will see how timely the recent entries are, look that key works have been included, and determine how shallow or deep the list goes. Do not overlook spending time on the reference list, both from a completeness and a format point-of-view.

A final reminder: track all the work you read and use along the way. Cite, cite, cite. All your work must be original and have no whiff of impropriety.

Plagiarism is an ugly word that can follow a writer or researcher for years, even if unfair or unfounded. Of course, there are the rare few who intentionally take whole tracts of text from others without giving credit. They are in large part the exceptions. Most "plagiarism" accusations are more connected with the author not properly citing a source. As you pull together the references related to your work, be mindful of leaving no question as to the ground on which your work is built.

Remember: strive to have all content in your presentation be original. Including material (a table, an image, some text) that comes from a third party (such as a peer review journal or monograph) will mean you must seek permission from the owner or publisher of that material. The process can slow down your efforts and there may be a fee (possibly a hefty one) to use the material. There certainly are some instances when you will need specific content from a source but try to minimize it. If you need to seek permission, start early. Also, never rely on the concept of fair use for any image, table, or long tract of text. "Grabbing something off a website" is never an acceptable strategy. When in doubt, cite the material and seek permission.

Chapter 14

Editing Your Work

Ask yourself at every moment, "Is this necessary?"
—Marcus Aurelius

REFINING YOUR WRITING

Let us take a big leap and assume you have done the hard work and written the first draft of your manuscript. This is not meant to gloss over this challenging and time-consuming task.

Assuming you have a first draft of the whole book, you will need to do some editing and revising. You might have one of two reactions to this next step. You may be of the type that once something is created and looks passable, you never want to see it again. You may want to get on to the next task or topic. Also, once it is set down on paper, it may feel overwhelming to make substantive changes.

Or you may be of the opposite camp—you may love to tinker. Add a comma here, fix a phrase there, add a thought here or there. You may like to edit so much that it is never final. You may want it perfect and feel it will never be good enough.

Editing and revising. Love it or hate it, you will need to come to grips with the importance of the task. Avoiding the revision process is common; just not productive. It takes a second and third and maybe fourth pass for you to catch what you missed when you created something the first time. If something sounds odd or out of place, it probably will be to your reader as well. Change it. Thinking that perfect prose rolls off your tongue onto the page that needs no correction is not reality-based. You will need to revise your material to make sure it is as good as it can be.

Conversely, if it is never perfect, and you always need just a little bit more time, you will never have a book. Or you will have an angry agent and publisher. Perfect and flawless is subjective. Your material will need to be looked at by other groups and your publisher. They are more objective and will be honest about what needs to change as opposed to you obsessively changing the manuscript. You need to produce a manuscript in a timely fashion, expect revisions, and then you will have a quality product that satisfies every party.

Reduce jargon. Inevitably, jargon creeps into almost all specialty or nonfiction work. Try to avoid it all costs. Think about your readers. They may not be as deeply invested in the field to know all the terminology. Also, spell out all abbreviations and acronyms at first mention.

Put your manuscript aside for a minimum of a week, or more, to put some distance between you and it. It will give you some perspective on your work.

The editing process is the perfect time to start to get feedback from other people about your work. This will help show you what needs to be improved. See the next chapter for advice on how to go about getting this input.

HEARING YOUR WRITING

One of the most important tips at this stage is reading your draft aloud. First, it refines your speaking skills. Second, it highlights weaknesses in the way some of your thoughts are expressed. As many people have pointed out, the written word is different from the spoken word.

If you do not want to read it aloud yourself, have your computer do it. Writers have some tremendous tools at their disposal. All of the major word processing software programs offer a read-aloud feature. This feature reads to you the text you have written. ReadAloud (Microsoft) offers a variety of voices (male and female) as well as different speeds. The narrator seems very, very close to normal speech. It has none of that robotic, jerky quality from years ago. This simple tool might be one of the most powerful (and underused) editing aspects of word processing software (Bond, 2022a).

USING A STYLE MANUAL

It is essential to understand the importance of style manuals. They can be extremely detailed and very specific. They run several hundred pages and give detailed information on such things as reference formatting, footnoting, table formation, and many other seemingly minute areas.

Style manuals can be valuable to beginning writers, as well as veterans. The correct use of one quickly illustrates whether authors are novice or veteran writers. They highlight the importance of consistency of style within a document. They show the author's ability to see their work as a whole rather than a collection of individual parts. Of course, professor should be capitalized when attached to a last name, such as Professor Bond. But when the word appears by itself in the text, should professor be capitalized? A style manual will weigh in on these and thousands of other details. They also serve as a refresher course for many areas of language that remain elusive to authors.

There are some very well-known style manuals:

- *The Chicago Manual of Style*
- *MLA Handbook*
- *AMA Manual of Style: A Guide for Authors and Editors*
- *Publication Manual of the American Psychological Association*

There are others. Likely at this point you know the style manual that is preferred in your subject area. Read and follow it closely, but any guidance your publisher gives you supersedes the manual (Bond, 2023a).

The editing stage is an opportunity to tinker with the title and description. It might be fine as is, but once you have a final manuscript you can assess whether the title represents the content and has enough punch.

The size of the task of writing your manuscript should not be minimized. It can exceed all the other tasks, or it can be an easier one. It will depend on your circumstances. Also, there are numerous, excellent books on the art and mechanics of writing. Some are listed in the bibliography at the end of this book. Consult them according to your needs and comfort level. These books provide a separate education on a crucial aspect of book publishing.

You are on a roll. Congratulate yourself on your remarkable headway.

Chapter 15

Getting Feedback from Reviewers

To avoid criticism, say nothing, do nothing, and be nothing.
—Elbert Hubbard

LISTENING TO FEEDBACK

As you finalize your manuscript, you will need to start to share your work with others. A whole mystique has arisen about this step. Some people are worried about it being bad luck before the manuscript is complete. Or an author may feel self-conscious about putting their friends and loved ones in an awkward position of having to say honest things about their work.

Start to feel comfortable with the process of sharing your work with others, first in a small circle, and then in an ever-expanding one. Talking about it and sharing it also helps to sharpen your presentation skills, and your own understanding of the material.

Take small increments of the manuscript, perhaps by chapter, and share it with your friends or coworkers. If the book is a monograph or textbook, sharing it with your colleagues is a must to ensure the quality of the material.

You will gradually get to the point where you will want or need to share the whole manuscript with several people. When you start sharing your material, let people know exactly what you are looking for. Let them know if you would like their general opinion, or whether you want them to only let you know about content errors or to check for grammar. Tell them if you would like them to make notes on the manuscript or just give you verbal feedback. Finally, give them a target date for when you would like their comments returned.

Many people will claim to welcome criticism, however, when it actually arrives, they may not embrace it. Criticism, constructive or otherwise, can be very valuable. When receiving it, you need to step away from it being about you or a value judgment on the work. Think about what you can learn from the comments. Positive or negative, there is something for you to take out of everyone's observations.

Be willing to step away from it and see it from a different perspective. Many times, authors will get so close to the material that they can miss what could be valuable improvements to the work.

When judging comments, it may be worthwhile to bounce the potential improvements off an ideal reader (as previously discussed) or a colleague you admire. Get their opinion on whether the change is for the better, or not.

Consider also giving a preliminary reading to an audience. Take a section of the book or a couple of chapters and do a reading to a small group of potential customers. Be open and up front as to what your motives are. Ask for feedback and suggestions. See if they follow your writing, or whether they think you are missing the mark. Listen closely to what everyone says.

If you are fortunate to have many people who will read your manuscript, you may start to develop conflicting suggestions—ones that, while valid, represent a departure from how you wrote the book. These comments may refer to the kind of book that reviewer would like. At some point, you will need to make a judgment call. You have a vision of your book. You have chosen to go down certain roads, while deciding not to go down others. The danger of taking everyone's suggestions is that the book becomes one written by committee. At some point, you will need to stick to your vision and proceed as you see fit.

Receiving lots of similar suggestions from multiple sources may indicate that a chapter (or several chapters) needs reworking. Be open to the possibility that a section needs to be scrapped, and that you may need to rewrite it. While never anyone's favorite choice, this option usually improves a book (Bond, 2023a).

OTHER SOURCES OF FEEDBACK

Joining writing groups is a very valuable step. These peers will read your work and give you generous feedback. It is worthwhile to embrace these groups, whether online or in person, and take full advantage of all they offer.

Depending on your background and skill set, you may want to consider having a professional give you feedback. There are countless people and companies that provide editorial services. These companies can be very helpful in increasing the quality of your manuscript. They can help with structure or presentation of your thoughts.

Editorial services come at a cost. You should know ahead of time exactly what those charges will be. If the company quotes by the hour, ask them for a range of the number of hours that it might take. Do not leave it open-ended. Also, remember that the publisher will be having someone edit it as well. Only take this step if you have concerns about your skill level in writing.

If your book will be self-published, it is a *must* to have a professional editor go through the manuscript. Authors get too close to the material to be adequate judges on the form and execution.

No matter what, look for the finished product to be of great quality that has had independent input from outsiders.

Remember that anyone who reviews the manuscript can potentially add an endorsement or testimonial to your growing list. Whether from someone of eminent stature or a colleague, even quotes such as, "The best book I have ever read on the topic —L. M., Langhorne, Pennsylvania," will catch someone's eye.

Chapter 16

Finalizing Your Manuscript

Do not plan for ventures before finishing what's at hand. —Euripides

PULLING IT ALL TOGETHER

Before we start to discuss the path to find a publisher, let us look at where your book writing process is.

- At this point, you have written your first draft and gone through several edits. Do not rush or minimize this process. Making your manuscript as tight as possible will pay dividends later.
- You showed your work to colleagues and friends who have given you feedback. You made some adjustments based on their comments.
- You have your references or bibliography and all of your high-quality photos, figures, and tables in place.
- Run a final spelling and grammar check. It seems like a simple idea but utilize the power of your word processing software's review option. It can help more than people believe.

As previously mentioned, unintended plagiaristic issues can cause big problems. There is valuable plagiarism-checking software available. Consider using this to note any issues of concern. A web search will list a range of options for plagiarism-checking software. Sometimes your authoring software (such as Grammarly) will offer this option. It may be built-in or available as a plug-in for an additional fee. If you work at a university, your library or department may subscribe to one of several services. Check with them. Some last items to confirm:

- If you used any material from an outside source, did you seek and receive permission? Make sure proper credit lines are included.
- Review your title, table of contents, and short/long descriptions of your work to check that they are still optimal.
- Review the reasons you wanted to publish, from chapter 1. Does anything need to be adjusted?

We will come back to your manuscript soon. But for now, are you ready to dive into the details of publishing? Let us go.

Part III

SELECTING A BOOK PUBLISHING MODEL

Chapter 17

Understanding Book Publishing

Knowledge is power. —*Francis Bacon*

THE PLUSES AND MINUSES OF PUBLISHING

Way back in chapter 7, we discussed the many routes into getting your book published. You can contact a publisher with an idea and no sample chapter or manuscript, and you might get a contract. You might do the same but with some sample chapters. Or you might write the whole book and then seek a publisher. Whichever one you choose, understanding book publishing is essential to good decision making.

Most people will have an opinion at this point to either pursue traditional publishing or self-publishing. Because you may lean one way at this time, be open to other possibilities. You can always reverse course and go the other direction. Or you might decide to simultaneously pursue both at the same time, hedging your bets.

Either way, let us take some time to dive into the details of both and what is involved with each option. Read all the chapters in this section, even if you have already decided on one. Factors in each chapter have implications for the other ones.

Many years ago when most people talked about publishing a book, they were referring to the traditional model. This meant creating a book proposal, finding an agent or a publisher directly, having the publisher agree to publish the book, submitting the work and having the publisher edit and print it; the publisher also dealt with marketing and distribution (or not), and then paid the author a royalty of about 10 percent of net sales.

This system made publishing an exclusive feat, or a frustrating one, depending on your perspective. The process had (and still has) a lot of mystery about it and seems more about who you know than the quality of the submission. Finding a legitimate agent seemed just as mysterious. It also did not guarantee finding a publisher. There was a now-antiquated version of self-publishing at the time called vanity publishing, but this was rare and not highly regarded.

Traditional publishing was the only game in town until recently. It has had its challenges, thanks to the rise of the self-publishing phenomena as well as the prominence of Amazon and the demise of many brick-and-mortar bookstores. Let us look at the pluses and minuses of traditional publishing and self-publishing.

The pluses of the traditional model are:

- The publisher takes care of all the various steps including editing, printing, warehousing, distribution, marketing, sales.
- The publisher has established relationships for distribution with bookstores and retailers.
- The result is usually a high-quality product, or at least an acceptable one.
- It lets the writer concentrate on being just that and does not saddle them with being a businessperson or salesperson.
- The author receives a royalty and has little to no upfront investment other than their time.
- Being published (versus self-published) brought greater esteem to the author.

The minuses of the traditional model are:

- The process is very secretive and difficult for outsiders to break into.
- Ninety percent of sales is a huge amount to give away for the work the publisher does (or does not) do.
- Many times, the book does not get much marketing after the first few weeks and the publisher may then give up or push the responsibility back on the author.

- There is a perception of the loss of control in the editing or finished product such as the cover design.
- The process from submission of idea to acceptance to published book sometimes can be a lengthy period of time.

While we are on this topic, let us look at the same list for self-publishing. The pluses of self-publishing are:

- Much greater control over the product and process. Who knows the book and market better than the author?
- The quality can be equal to that of the largest companies.
- The amount received by the author per sale can be dramatically higher.
- It can be a very short period of time from idea to publication—instant gratification.

The minuses of self-publishing are:

- The author sometimes does not seek or accept outside counsel on critical issues. The result can be poor quality covers, illustrations, book titles, or marketing resulting in an amateurish product or presentation.
- The process, if done right, can become more expensive than antici-pated. If done cheaply, it can lead to an inferior result.
- Understanding the rules of the road of Amazon or getting your books in a bookstore takes time and energy.
- And, most unfortunately, most self-published authors lose steam after the product is released and do not market the book as much as they should or at all. This results in low sales and disappointment (Bond, 2018).

Getting back to traditional publishing—it continues to be a major force in publishing today and will be for the foreseeable future. Many still see this as the Holy Grail, particularly if an author signs with one of the larger publishers like Penguin Random House or Simon & Schuster.

This section of the book will start with the steps on how to go about getting traditionally published, namely: writing a book proposal, find-ing a publisher or finding an agent, securing a contract, and dealing with the publisher through the production process. Then the section will move on to the steps in self-publishing, including how self-publishing differs from traditional publishing.

Please read this whole section before you lean one way or another.

Chapter 18

Considering Self-Publishing

Freedom is the greatest fruit of self-sufficiency. —Epicurus

THE MODEL OF SELF-PUBLISHING

Perhaps traditional publishing is not the option for you. Maybe it is the difficulty of finding an agent or a publisher. Maybe it is the control that the publisher has over the process and the final product. Or is it the control you want to have over your own book? Maybe it is the low royalty rate compared to the lion's share of the sale price that goes to the publisher. Whatever the reason, let us look at self-publishing.

Self-publishing requires an author to not just write a book but to also serve in other roles. The self-published author becomes head salesperson, marketeer, and publicist as well. Some of these roles should feel natural to an author, such as selling. It is your book. Show your passion. Other roles may feel like a stretch. Nonetheless, self-publishing to many has felt liberating, making them directors of their own fate.

The model of self-publishing has gelled a lot over the past ten years, but it can still feel like the Wild West to new authors. Understand the expectations and the "rules" and make an informed decision about what is best for you.

Be heartened by the success stories. Many people know *The Martian* (Andy Weir). The bestselling novel started as a self-published title. Search online for "Self-Publishing Success Stories" for inspiration.

Fiction authors definitely have the advantage here, but nonfiction has a good case to be made as well. Despite these stratospheric successes, go into it with realistic or modest expectations to start.

Self-publishing requires more of a flair for marketing and promotion. If you are not detail-oriented and do not like selling, do not self-publish.

Control is what attracts many people to this option. They can decide on their own cover. They can choose the paper the book will be printed on. They can determine who will get to hear about their book, and who will not. However, even with self-publishing, some issues are still out of your control. You cannot control whether a retailer or store chooses to carry your book.

Keeping most of the money from a sale makes greater sense to many people, instead of being paid a royalty of 10 percent or so. However, with all those sales come other costs. Will you use a freelance editor? Who will design the cover? Should you use Google Ads? All of these options (and many, many more) do not come free. Plus, there is all of your time to manage or perform all these tasks.

Self-publishing, for it to be effective, has to be a labor of love. If all you want to do is concentrate on writing in your subject area, this may not be the option for you.

On the positive side, you will probably be able to create your product much sooner than the twelve to eighteen months publishers can take once they get a finished manuscript. Also, self-publishing may lead to working with a publisher. If you are successful, it is not unheard of to have a publisher approach you about buying the book's rights or wanting to publish your next book. If this happens, your track record will put you on much firmer footing to discuss equitable financial arrangements.

Since some self-publishers emphasize the eBook option, the barrier to entry can be lower. Some authors can accomplish this very quickly if they are less worried about printing and storage and order fulfillment. With the proliferation of eReaders in dedicated devices like the Kindle, smartphones, and tablets, almost anybody can be reading anytime, anywhere.

The steps in self-publishing are as follows (many of which mirror traditional publishing):

- Confirm concept. Create the title and preliminary description.
- Write the book. Have it read and reviewed by others.

- Get an editor and book designer.
- Get great endorsements or testimonials.
- Have a great cover created.
- Decide if it will be a paper book, eBook, or both. Confirm proper file format.
- Find a publishing partner or distribution partner (more on this later).
- Create an Author Promotional Platform and a Marketing and Promotional Plan.
- Write the marketing description for the book. Consider getting outside help.
- Send the book to the printer/upload the file to the partner platform.
- Publish the book!
- Ramp up the marketing and promotion. And never let up (Bond, 2018).

Many of these steps have a chapter in this book, either in the traditional publishing section or still to come. Review all of them closely.

Most of these tasks should not be done sequentially; that is write the manuscript, then arrange for a distributor, then set up your company and so on. They will need to be done in concert with each other. Start to make lists of the different tasks that need to happen. As these lists emerge, start to arrange them in order and assign target dates to start them and have them completed.

There are some excellent books that take the budding self-publisher from soup to nuts. These books address many of the business matters that need not be addressed in this book. Buy these books and let them guide you through the process.

DISTRIBUTION IS ESSENTIAL

The key part of self-publishing (and publishing for that matter) is distribution. Having your eBook or paper book available through Amazon and other online retailers or brick-and-mortar stores is critical. Most self-publishers need this help. Do not try to do it yourself. Perhaps you just need a partner for trade distribution. Like it or not, experts estimate Amazon could be as high as 50 percent of the print book market and 70 percent of the eBook market. You will need a partner to make your work available to Amazon on their terms. So, what do these partners do?

The first option is just distribution. Perhaps you want to do it all yourself: get an editor and cover designer, get files converted, do the marketing. You just need a company to connect your eBook or paper copy to Amazon and other retailers.

The second option is a company that offers publishing services and distribution. These companies can help with the component pieces of publishing as well as distribution. You might also hear the term aggregator or eBook aggregator. These provide much of the same service as a distributor for eBooks.

The business models for these companies all vary, as do their services. Some will work off a flat fee for the services, others off a percentage of any sale you make. Some vary in their percentage based on print versus eBook, others by region or sales channel.

Kindle Direct Publishing, IngramSpark, Smashwords, BookBaby, and others provide some menu of services. Sometimes you can work with two of these companies for greater effect, such as working with Smashwords and Amazon. A list of possible partners is included in the "Resources" section at the end of the book.

Be aware that in other areas, a phenomenon has arisen called predatory publishing. Companies charge to publish a peer review journal article and provide no value or legitimacy to what they do, other than posting a word processing version of the article at a website no one visits. There is no exact parallel in book publishing, but there are companies that provide shoddy service or continue to add to their fees after you have committed to them. With any self-publishing partner, do your research ahead of time.

Educating yourself, particularly with self-publishing, is essential. If you choose to self-publish, please do yourself a favor and research the nuances between all of these distribution services very, very closely. Look at their terms and conditions. Search the Web for advice from other self-publishers. Read online forums from actual users. Filter your search so you only see answers within the last year to ensure they are up to date. Consider carefully all your options before you make any final decision.

Minimally consider these companies (Kindle Direct Publishing or KDP, IngramSpark, Smashwords) before you sign up with any newer, boutique service. There are other good ones out there. Just be fully informed.

These services (or likely a combination of them) will help you turn your manuscript into a finished print book or eBook, as well as make it available online at Amazon and other online retailers.

At the end of the day, be educated about self-publishing. Do your research and ask a lot of questions.

Chapter 19

Finding a Publisher

Seek and you shall find. —*The Bible, Matthew 7:7*

CHOOSING THE TYPE

You are at a fork in the road. You have decided to go with traditional publishing, compared to self-publishing. Will you find a publisher directly, or seek an agent? For this chapter, let us assume you are going to look for a publisher directly. If you are looking to publish a textbook, monograph, or technical/specialty work, this is probably the best path. Agents are less necessary for these types of work. Remember, your decision is not set in stone, and therefore can be revisited after reading these chapters.

There are different types of publishers from big to small, general to specialized. Think about your motives, your personality type, and your material.

Are you interested in significant royalties? Then maybe you need to concentrate on the largest New York publishers. The largest firms find the vast majority of all the books they publish via agents.

Is your work a technical one? Your list of possible publishers may be very narrow, which is not necessarily a bad thing.

Will a lot of marketing be done via your own efforts, such as speaking engagements? Then maybe a smaller publisher will work just as well.

Do you have a lot of connections in your geographic area? Then a regional publisher might work best.

After you have thought about the type of publisher you are interested in seeking, you will next need to come up with a list of publishers in that category. You will also need to determine the best way to be in contact with them.

Literary Market Place (LMP) is a valuable reference. This website lists all publishers with their contact information and some other valuable facts. Libraries may have access to the website or a print version. There are other great websites with lists of publishers, but some require a fee (as does LMP); others may not be complete. There are thousands of publishers, and it is tough to tell one from another after a while. They all sound like possibilities.

You will need to narrow down the publishers you want to contact. There are several methods for coming up with your best prospects. One of the best ways is to look for books in the same field or genre as yours. Go to a large bookstore or library. Browse the section where your book would be located. Look for books published in the last two to four years. Librarians and bookstore managers have a wealth of knowledge. Most likely you will start to notice some of the same publishers over and over.

If you come across a book that is directly competing against yours, take note. The publisher may choose not to publish your book because it might create competition with itself. This is not always true, but this may be a factor you want to consider.

A good rule of thumb is that first-time authors should lean toward small- or medium-sized publishers for their first book. You are more likely to find one and more apt not to get lost in their system. There are exceptions, but this may help to guide some of your decisions.

RANKING YOUR PROSPECTS

Make a list beginning with the best prospects, ranking them by desirability. Limit the list to twenty or fewer prospects. You may not even get to twenty. As you find better candidates, your list will change, and some may be replaced by better matches. Also remember that some publishers may have merged or changed focus.

You should also look at trade publications. *Publisher's Weekly* is an essential website/magazine for book publishing. It contains information on who is doing what and what they are publishing. It has valuable articles on publishing, sometimes gives editors' names, and often discusses agents.

There are other, more creative ways to find publishers. Networking with writers, agents, or large bookstore managers is a good one. Do not be afraid to ask a favor of a new acquaintance. There are also large gatherings or conventions where publishers are located. They may be geared toward book publishers, booksellers, or librarians. You do not need to attend them as they can be expensive or limit who can participate. But the list of participating or exhibiting publishers (which is usually available online) can be a good source of leads.

Work ruthlessly to match your book to the appropriate publishers. Nothing is a bigger waste of your time (and the publisher's) than to receive a proposal for a subject or format of book they would never consider publishing.

REACHING OUT TO THE RIGHT PERSON

Take your list and go to the LMP or similar database and look up each publisher's entry. Make sure you have the right email address and contact information. The LMP lists key personnel for each publisher. Some publishers will list editors to whom material should be addressed. Even if it does not list the contact person for book proposals, it can put you in touch with some people worth talking to. Most importantly, and perhaps the best alternative to the LMP, is to go to the publisher's website. Most times, their sites are geared toward publicizing or selling books, but many will have information on how to submit a proposal. Read carefully what they request that you do and stick to it.

You are now set to contact the publisher. You might send your proposal or a query letter (more on these to come), depending on the publisher's preference or your type of project. The query letter is a hybrid of your cover letter and the overview section of your proposal. It queries the person on their interest in seeing the full proposal. Limit the query letter to one page, maximum. Important notes to hit in a query letter (to a publisher or an agent) are a brief but engaging explanation of the book; why it is right for them; who you are; why it is different from what is on the market and why the market wants it; length; and timeline.

Always, always address your email to a specific person. Never address the letter to "Dear Sir or Madam" or "To whom it may concern." If you do not have an exact name from your research, call the company and ask for the editorial department. Ask to whom submissions should be addressed. Or do deep research on the Web. LinkedIn is particularly helpful.

You will want to respect any request a publisher may have on simultaneous submissions. This is when agents or publishers look at proposals at the same time. Many times, publishers or agents will request that they be the sole group looking at your material. If you do not know a publisher's policy, assume it prefers not to receive simultaneous submissions. This will require you to keep track of when you submit to a publisher, and to follow up in a timely manner and to ask for feedback. If they are nonresponsive after an acceptable time period (perhaps one to two months), you can then proceed to your next candidate. If you do choose to send simultaneous submissions, make sure to note this in your cover letter.

Not all books at all publishers are bought through agents. The smaller the publisher or the more specialized the topic, the less likely this is to be the case.

When you contact publishers, you may be dealing with editors or acquisitions editors. Acquisitions editors are charged with finding and signing new projects. After you have a contract, the editor may continue to be your key contact for a period of time, but you will get to know other people as well. When an editor or acquisitions editor begins to develop an interest in your project, they will need approval from other people at the publisher. This may be an editorial committee, probably composed of people in management, finance, marketing, and production (Bond, 2018).

UNDERSTANDING REJECTION

Rejection has become part of the whole mystique of being an author. People react in different ways, but the most common response one hears is dejection or disappointment. Sure, it would be great if your first, best choice agreed to publish your book on the first try, but that is not always the case. Rejection does not mean your work is bad or you are unqualified.

Even if it is a form letter, do not read too much into a rejection letter, or even several of them. There can be innumerable reasons for being rejected, many having nothing to do with you or your work. Often you will not know the true reason for the rejection. The publisher may have recently agreed to publish a book on the same topic. Or they may have exceeded the number of titles they planned to publish in a year. You may have caught them on an off day when nothing looked appropriate for their line of books. Or you may have done a poor job of matching the publisher with the topic. Do not go to a hardware store for a frying pan. Sure, they may have it, but you would be better off going to a home goods store. The same is true when "shopping" for a publisher. Match your project to the best publishing house and their interests.

Move on from the rejection and keep trying. If you are lucky enough to get personal feedback about your proposal or idea, carefully consider whether to adjust your work based on such feedback. Try to be objective, while staying true to your vision of your project. Stay persistent. You will prevail, and someone will agree to publish your work.

At this point in the process, you probably just want a publisher or an agent. But if given the choice, what you want is one with certain qualities or characteristics:

- Top of the list is enthusiasm for your project. Your excitement for the book should carry over to them.
- A publisher (or agent) should have worked with other books in your field, which demonstrates knowledge of the area, and a commitment to it.
- You want a publisher (or agent) that answers you in a timely manner.
- Finally, you want a publisher that feels you are the person to write the book.

Granted, a publisher or agent that does not have all of these qualities may do. If they do not, your happiness at the prospect of being published now may be tempered by some harsh realities later.

Chapter 20

Finding an Agent

It is a great piece of skill to know how to guide your luck even while waiting for it. —Baltasar Gracián

WHAT IS AN AGENT AND WHAT DO THEY DO?

Do I need an agent? It is a common question people ask on their publishing journey. It may appear unnecessarily time-consuming or complex. Whether you *need* one or not depends. Obviously, if you are self-publishing, this is a nonissue. In most specialized areas, such as textbook and monograph publishing, agents are usually not part of the normal process. What makes many people wary of finding representation is the previously mentioned catch-22. How do I find an agent if they only represent published authors, and how can I get published if I do not have an agent? Do not despair. Most agents need first-time authors, just not as much as first-time authors need agents.

Having an agent will make your quest for a publisher easier and publication more successful. The vast majority of agents are interested in people who present themselves well, understand and are serious about their ideas, understand marketing, have a platform to connect with readers, and have a polished proposal or manuscript.

Let us start with a common question: what do agents actually do? First and foremost, an agent should get your proposal looked at by the right people in the right publishing houses. For this service alone, they are worth their fee. Instead of spending a lot of time floundering around and learning through rejection, an agent will be able to assess your idea and, if they are interested, marry it to the right publisher.

The agent knows who is buying and in what area. They should also be objective, which may not be to an author's liking. Agents ask and answer the right questions. They have been through the process many times and know why things are the way they are. They can educate you about the various aspects of publishing. On the opposite end, the agent will be the intermediary with the publisher with your requests, questions, or concerns.

The agent can run interference, either way, with difficult issues. After the agent gets your manuscript placed with a publisher and gets you a contract, their role will change. They will move from selling you and your idea to helping facilitate manuscript submission and, ultimately, to publication.

At the top of the list of what agents get credit for is the financial deal. They may help you get a bigger advance or higher royalty. How far the financial issue can be pushed can, in and of itself, earn you back what an agent is paid. If you are an unpublished author and can get an agent, the services they will provide are probably invaluable to you although you may not yet realize it.

FINDING AN AGENT

But how do you find an agent? Many of the suggestions or tactics in the previous chapter on finding a publisher will apply to agents as well. The LMP lists the largest, most well-known agencies that do not need to advertise their services or existence.

There are some worthy websites to consider. Publishers Marketplace is probably the most respected of the website databases. QueryTracker helps authors find agents or publishers as well as track their efforts. AgentQuery offers "one of the largest searchable databases of literary agents on the web." There may be fees associated with the full uses of some of these sites.

There are at least a couple of sites that use the form of a wish list, connecting authors with agent's needs (Manuscript Wish List and MS WishList). See the resources for links to all these sites. Also, hashtags have become a good way to connect with agents such as #AskAgent or #querytip or #MSWL.

A common way to find agents is to look in the acknowledgments in a book. Look in books that are in the field in which you hope to publish. Many times, authors will thank their agent by name and sometimes by agency. If an author thanks an agent just by name, put the name into a search engine and see what comes up.

You can also email an author and ask them to refer you to their agent or agency. If this happens, make sure you note this in the first sentence of your email to the agent.

Also, networking can be invaluable. Going to writers' conferences or seminars are ways to meet people who have agents. Briefly tell them your idea and background. Ask authors if they can suggest someone or if they know someone else to ask.

Take note of who the agent is and what they have done. Who they represent (specifically in your area of expertise) and how many books they successfully placed will tell you whether they are worth their salt.

Unfortunately, anyone can call themselves an agent, but it does not mean they will be able to find a publisher for your book. Beware, an inferior agent is worse than no agent. An inferior agent is one who is not respected by publishers or one who cannot get books placed with appropriate publishers. Potentially, you can ask for a list of references to ensure that your agent cuts the mustard.

Whenever possible, try to find an agent who is a member of the Association of Authors' Representatives. This nonprofit organization also provides a "Find an Agent" feature. While admirable, this is a voluntary group that at this point contains 400 agents and is not a comprehensive list, but it is a good place to start.

All of these suggestions come with a caution. Agents that are big and successful do not need the publicity. Those that are struggling and just starting may generate a lot of buzz to pull you in. Beware (Bond, 2018).

CONTACTING AGENTS

Once you have developed a list of potential agents, you will need to decide whether to send a query letter or a letter and the full proposal. LMP recommends a query with an outline and a sample chapter. You may be able to check what an agent prefers by looking in LMP or on their website. For others, it may not be readily apparent what is preferred. In these instances, start with the proposal. As with the publishers, observe any requests they may have not to receive simultaneous submissions. If you do send query letters simultaneously, note it in the letter.

When looking at your cover letter, or the query letter that you created, make sure it is adjusted to the agent's point of view, as opposed to the publisher's. The agent wants to know that you are committed to the project, have the ability to promote the book, and will follow through on your commitments.

After a few weeks, feel free to contact the person to whom you sent the materials. As with a publisher, after a reasonable period of time without a response, it is acceptable to move on to another potential agent. With agents and publishers, track to whom you sent your materials and on what date. You do not want to duplicate your efforts.

Most agents will get 15 percent of everything you are paid. This includes an advance, your royalty payment, rights payments for other uses, and so on. There are exceptions to these percentages, but as a rough guideline, 15 percent is a good ballpark figure. For those of you who are skeptical about how hard an agent works for you, remember that 15 percent of nothing is nothing. Most agents (unless they are charging you fees to read your manuscript) get no money if they never place your book.

WHAT YOU OWE AN AGENT

Aside from the money, you owe the agent several things. You owe the agent your honest and open consideration of their suggestions and ideas. They are a neutral party and, many times, know best. If an agent makes a suggestion, you owe it to them to listen very carefully and consider the idea. You also need to be honest, whether it is regarding a delivery date or your ability to meet the request of the publisher.

The agent owes you several things. As mentioned in the previous chapter, agents should be enthusiastic about your project. The agent needs to have a good knowledge and a track record in your area. Finally, the agent needs to return your calls or emails in a timely manner.

You will sign a contract with your agent. It will be shorter than the one you will sign with your publisher. More on the publishing contract later. Your contract with your agent gives your permission for the publisher to deal with the agent on financial and other matters. It will state that all payments and reports will go to the agent. It will formalize the relationship you have with the agent. Read any agreement with an agent and consider whether you should have a (knowledgeable) attorney review it as well.

An important caution—some agents in the industry use fees to offset costs or to actually make money. Some may charge reading fees to look at your proposal or manuscript. There may be more fees in addition to these, with no guarantee that you will receive a contract if their edits are made. It is generally agreed that agents who stress these fees or have very high fees are really only offering editorial services and are not agents. Most agents want to make money from the percentage of the advance or royalty, as opposed to just charging reading fees.

Unless you are paying an editor for a critique of your manuscript, never pay an agent for any service other than their commission for book sales. In fact, run from anyone that asks. Finally, there are many publishers who will not even accept or review unagented manuscripts or proposals.

In conclusion, if you have the opportunity to proceed down the road to getting a publisher with or without an agent, get one. An agent's efforts, while costing you a percentage of your royalty, will almost always make the process go better and more smoothly. Agents know the industry and will provide valuable assistance to you as you navigate a unique landscape.

Chapter 21

Creating a Book Proposal and Query Letter

We are what we think. All that we are arises with our thoughts. With our thoughts, we make the world. —*Buddhist teaching*

THE PARTS OF A BOOK PROPOSAL

A great book proposal is the foundation of all the other work you have done. It will help you to continue to focus on what your book is about. It will help you secure a publisher or an agent. A well-written proposal is the roadmap for others to understand your project. It will give your promotional and marketing efforts direction. If you self-publish, it is your business plan. It will help you to stay focused and provide you with guidance.

This step may take some time, but it will prove to be time well spent. Do not rush the process or settle for a less-than-perfect proposal. Also, remember to use colleagues and friends to review your draft proposal and letter. This task is equally valuable at this stage. When you are finished, have multiple people give you feedback on the proposal, in particular the overview, before you submit it to anyone.

Think of the proposal as a means of selling your project with you as the author and not as a way of describing your project to a potential publisher.

A well-done proposal includes all of the following parts, in the listed order (with a target length for each):

- *Title Page:* Includes the title of your book, as well as your contact information (name, address, phone, cell phone, and email address). (Half page)
- *A Proposed Table of Contents:* Lists the items in the proposal with their page numbers. Make sure you add page numbers to each page of the proposal. (Half page)
- *Overview:* This is your opportunity (perhaps the only one) to sell your project. It includes a concise and enticing description of the book. The genesis of this should be the three-paragraph description of the book that you have already created, the difference being the style in which it is written. You will need a hook or a way to instantly grab the reader's attention. Draw them in. Present your USP or unique selling proposition that tells readers why your book is perfect for them or what separates it from other books on the same topic. Think about what need your book fulfills. The language and power of this section is most important. You will end it with a brief physical description of the book you want to write. An example is: "My manuscript will be 400 pages, with 15 photographs. I envision the final book being 6" X 9", soft cover, 250 pages." (Three to six pages)
- *About the Author:* This gives you the opportunity to say why you are *the* person to write the book. Extol your background. Talk about your accomplishments. Do not be shy. Include as much information as necessary to establish you as the expert you are. (One page)
- *Schedule:* Talk about when you can deliver the completed manuscript. Be pessimistic. Under-promise and over-deliver. If you have written the whole manuscript already, now is the time to brag about it. (One paragraph)
- *Resources Needed:* May be optional. If you need certain assistance or funding, this allows you the opportunity to make that known. The less you request, the better off you are. However, if you cannot get the book done without these resources, the publisher will need to know this up front. (One paragraph)
- *Competition:* An extremely important component, this section details the books someone might buy instead of yours. Present a bulleted list starting with a bibliographic entry for each book, and then a brief reason why yours is better or different. Use Amazon, other online retailers, a web search, and other websites to find out who the competition is. Use customer reviews to bolster your analysis. Remember,

everyone thinks their idea is unique. Here is your chance to prove it. Shy away from saying, "there is nothing like my book." As you look at competitive books, note which ones are in multiple editions (a sure sign of success). Some bestselling books prominently proclaim right on the front cover how they are doing. "Over 1,000,000 copies in print" is a great quote to use. Only present in-print books as competition, not out-of-print books. Shoot to have at least three to six books. (Two to four pages)

- *The Market:* You will need to explain who the market for your book is. The more facts and statistics you can use, the better. In most cases, concentrate your facts on the United States. Professional associations, trade groups, the United States Bureau of the Census, or the US Bureau of Labor Statistics can be *very* helpful in providing market data. The publisher will create a tentative profit-and-loss statement for the book. Why not make this process easier (and your acceptance more likely) by providing the information on market size? (One to two pages)

- *Author Promotional Platform:* A publisher will want to know what activities are necessary to sell the book—more on this in chapter 30. This does not mean they will agree with it, but it allows the publisher to gauge what you feel will make the book a success. You will also list what activities you plan on creating or participating in. It is part of the publishing industry's expectation that the author will not create a book and then wash their hands of it. A publisher will want to know that the author may be speaking about the book or may have a website that features the book or will buy copies for resale to the author's contacts or customers. A strong Author Promotional Platform with significant commitments by the author can be very influential in making a potential publisher interested. (Two to three pages)

- *Table of Contents:* This is your polished version, with an exact listing of the number of chapters and chapter titles. If the book changes when you write it from twelve to thirteen chapters, the publisher will not care. The publisher *will* care if the manuscript goes from 300 to 600 pages. Be diligent in making sure you have the natural order of the material and what will be covered. Other changes may occur; do not sweat it. Just make sure the publisher is apprised of them. (One to two pages)

- *Chapter Outline:* This gives a description of each chapter. Do not brush this off. Spend the proper time with it. This outline could be a highly influential factor in someone deciding whether or not to pursue the book. (Two to five pages)
- *Sample Chapter(s):* Depending on the market, you will need to submit approximately one-tenth of the book. Choose those chapters that are most representative of the book or that show the material in its best light. These chapters will allow the reader to see your style. Are you coming from a folksy approach or a just-the-facts style? It will also allow the publisher to see if you are presenting material in depth or just touching on the highlights. (About 25 pages) (Bond, 2018)

THE COVER OR QUERY LETTER

The proposal is critical, but before a publisher or agent gets to the proposal, they see the cover letter first. The cover letter is different from a query letter, which is sent by itself without a proposal.

Query letters are normally associated with trying to find an agent. Some publishers prefer query letters. At the end of the day, you will check with the potential agent or publisher's website which will specify if they want a query first, or a cover letter and proposal, or perhaps some sample chapters.

The cover or query letter have much of the same goals: to introduce you and your project in a brief, enticing way. The conclusion will vary in that you will note what might be attached (a proposal and/or sample chapters) or offer to send such materials.

The cover letter to the proposal plays an important role. Many people will scan it and then proceed to the main course without having spent much time with it. However, some people may scrutinize the letter to save the time of having to read the proposal. Write the cover letter as if someone may never see the proposal. Write it as if these four or five paragraphs are your only opportunity to talk with a potential agent or publisher.

The opening sentence and paragraph may be a hybrid of your overview from the proposal. Tease or challenge the reader to such an extent that the reader will want to read the proposal. Keep the letter short and succinct but include enough facts about the book in case the reader wants to know what it is you are pitching.

Quality is one of the hallmarks of success. Authors talk about why their book is better than the competition. Treat the proposal the same way. Make sure you put maximum effort into creating the proposal. Write, revise, refine. Test it out on many people. Ask them what they would change, or where their interest wanes.

Even if your book is on a technical subject, the proposal should be able to be read and understood by most people. Use a minimal amount of jargon in the proposal, unless it is absolutely necessary to convey what you will cover.

This is also a good time to revisit your title. Now that you have further defined the book, you can examine your title to make sure it is a winner and reflects your current direction. Make any necessary refinements.

There are some excellent books on writing a proposal. Some are listed in the bibliography. Read more about this crucial step.

Remember, publishing is a business interested in making money. Publishers are not altruists. You will need to appeal to their business side about the sales your project will generate.

Finally, be truthful and do not exaggerate. Making your market sound much larger or wildly exaggerating the book's potential may cause other statements you make to be dismissed.

You have created a dynamic proposal—what next? There are some small details that are very important.

Have several people proofread it simply for grammar and spelling. Nothing will diminish your credibility like misspelled words. Before it goes anywhere, double-check that it is picture perfect. Like résumés for job hunting, the person receiving your submission is looking to eliminate the amateurs who make obvious mistakes, like forgetting a component.

People wonder if they should copyright their proposal. No need to do this in my experience. Others ask what prevents publishers or agents from taking their idea and giving it to their favorite writers. For nonfiction work, this issue is just flattery of the person asking the question since there are few unique ideas in publishing.

Very few people have such groundbreaking work that has not been done by someone else in some other way, or some other area. They may think it so, but it is most likely not true. The overwhelming majority of publishers' and agents' greatest asset is their good name and reputation. Stealing ideas would damage their asset. Plus, if the publisher is going to pay a royalty on the work, they are not saving any money giving your idea to someone else. If anything, it may cost them in legal fees. Worry more about making your proposal and book as dynamic as possible, instead of worrying about someone stealing your secret formula.

Despite the previous point, your proposal should be so complete that a creative person who is an expert in the field should be able to take your proposal and write a similar book. Granted it would be a different book and would not have your mark on it, but it would be close. Hold nothing back from the proposal. Put it all on the line.

You now have a dynamic proposal. Sit back for a moment and look at the progress you have made. Finding a publisher is in sight. But before you do this, it will be very beneficial if you find testimonials from well-known people in your field.

Chapter 22

Getting Endorsements
for Your Book

Neither blame or praise yourself. —Plutarch

SIX DEGREES OF SEPARATION

Just think if you got Oprah to say the following about your self-help book: "It changed my life." Or how about if the president of General Motors said, "The ideas in this book will revolutionize global business." Or if Rachel Ray exclaimed, "This book taught me more about cooking than anything else in life." It does not hurt to dream.

For many books, testimonials or endorsements can be the difference between success and mediocrity or getting published versus having your manuscript sit in a drawer. Imagine the instant credibility you would have with a potential publisher or agent if you could include in your cover letter or proposal a guarantee that you could get a national radio talk show host or a Pulitzer Prize–winner (or the appropriate top person in your field) to write a glowing foreword to the book.

Instead of scoffing in disbelief, the only thing stopping you is yourself, some research, and time. People are always surprised to find out two facts. First, almost everyone knows someone who knows or has met someone very, very famous. This is where the concept of six degrees of separation originated. Second, they are amazed at just how common it is for mid-level famous people to agree to write a few sentences about your work. These people probably remember the past when they were trying to climb the ladder as well.

Other than the time spent on your proposal, this step is one of the most essential tasks not to rush. If successful, it can be very influential when trying to find a publisher or agent. More time spent here will increase the chances of you getting published as well as selling more books later. As the Disneyland chorus sings, "It's a small world after all."

Perhaps you realize that you know the leaders in your field. Many people do not know just how well connected they are. If you do not, it is time to think about who you know and who *they* know. Six degrees of separation has become a part of cultural lore. It started with a study about forty years ago. People in the Midwest were asked to have something delivered to a person in Boston unknown to them. When asked to do this, they found someone, who knew someone, who knew them. With the advent of the internet, people estimate the degrees of separation are now down to three!

Most people do not know Barack Obama, Anthony Fauci, or Stephen King. However, most people have well over 1,000 connections, considering family, friends, work, neighbors, and so on. Each of those people has connections as well and so on. You can see how quickly the circle spreads.

Start to make a list of the people you know who are connected to your topic area. Some people will be very well connected while others not. Do not overlook the latter, as they only need to know one or two key people to get out of the bounds of their small circle of friends and potentially reach someone important.

Think about what someone does, where they have lived, and what stories they have told over the years.

Keep making your list. Concentrate on the people who work in higher-profile jobs or those who work outside your circle. You may just want to list people to talk to, so you can find out who they know or have met. They may surprise you.

ASKING FAVORS

The biggest challenge you will face is not wanting to ask friends or neighbors a favor. Maybe it has to do with not imposing on them or maybe you do not want to discuss your dream of publishing a book with them. However, you will need to get past it. Overcoming this hesitancy will be key to your success.

As your list expands, you need to continue to concentrate on your subject area. If you are writing a book on needlepoint, you do not need George W. Bush or Tom Hanks to write a blurb. Maybe your list is easy because you are looking for the titans of your specialty field. Even if you just need the big names of your field, still shoot as high as you can.

Think also about professional or trade associations or groups that work in your area. Having the director of NASCAR write a blurb for your book on the history of racetracks in the United States would be at the top of your list. Finally, do not leave off businesses. The leaders of the businesses in your field will lend credibility, depending on the topic.

Think about who would best serve your interest to write a blurb or the foreword. Only one person can write the foreword to the book. Many people, however, can write an endorsement or blurb (two or three sentences giving their opinion about the content) about the book. Reserve your grandest wish or biggest name for the foreword. Remember, you will excerpt whatever they say and put it on the back cover as well. An excerpt will also go into your proposal and cover letter.

You should also target people who are connected to your topic to comment on the book for use on the front cover, back cover, and the first two pages of the book where the endorsements or testimonials are typically listed, as well as in any marketing materials.

Have them comment on you as the author, the content and its quality, or their take on the work as a whole and its importance. On rare occasions, someone may ask the type of comments you want. Feel free to submit a sample of what you are looking for. If this happens, be positive but not outlandish.

The tasks discussed in this chapter can be worked on or accomplished before the proposal stage, or when the manuscript is completed.

Doing it early allows you to use these actual endorsements, or agreements to do one, to gain a publisher. If it is done at a later stage when the manuscript is completed, you will have a greater number of people agreeing to a review based on being able to see the actual book.

HOW TO ASK

How to ask is as important as whom to ask. If you have a passing acquaintance with the person, a phone call will be best. If you came by them from someone you know very well directly, perhaps you could ask the person to make an introductory call, with you following up after that.

When (and if) you get the person on the phone, be quick and to the point. You recently wrote a book (or are in the process of writing one), and you would be honored if the person would preview it. If it meets with their approval, any comments would be greatly appreciated.

Offer to send the complete book/manuscript or sample chapters. For all people who agree to write a blurb or the foreword, you will need to secure written permission to use the comments in print as well as the person's name and affiliation.

If you only know the person who is introducing you in a peripheral way, a letter or email will probably be better. Mention the mutual acquaintance in the first sentence. If you receive no response in two weeks or so, you should follow up with a phone call. Mention immediately that you are following up on your letter/email and also again note the person's name who knows them.

If the person has agreed to look at it, send the material as soon as possible. Ask them if they would prefer an electronic or paper copy. Include a letter that reminds the person about your conversation, what it is you want, and that the person agreed to look at it.

If the person is reviewing the idea, your proposal, or a section of the book prior to completion, offer to send a complete copy when you are done. Or perhaps have the reviewer agree to review it when complete. This promise will be extremely valuable to include in your proposal.

Do not be discouraged by people not returning your calls or saying no. Perseverance is the name of the game. Ask, ask, ask. What is the worst that can happen? That they say no? So what?

Most people are apt to give up too soon. The only exception is if you came by this contact via a personal friend and if the person you are asking is a close associate of theirs. Do not put your friend in an awkward position of having the person you are asking unhappy with having their name passed along.

WHO TO ASK

Persistence will win the day in many cases. Another strategy to use, if you ask someone and the person says no, is to ask who that person can recommend who may be able to do it. If you asked the president of Coca-Cola to comment on your new business strategy book and they said no, maybe they will suggest that the vice president might want to do it. It would not be a bad second place. When this happens, mention that the first person suggested you contact them. Their name will surely catch their attention.

A key point is the importance of getting the right contact information. Many times, people do not respond because they did not receive the requests. Do your research as to what is the best way to reach someone. Most famous people have their own websites, like https://stephen king.com/. See if the site provides a way to contact the person. Or look in their books and see where they live. A quick search may provide contact information. Do not contact them by phone unless you have a personal connection to them. Many times, sending your query to an intermediary, like their publisher, can prove fruitful, or it may mean they are screening their correspondence. When in doubt, send it to multiple sources.

If you have secured a publisher or agent, they can be a great source of contacts for quality candidates to write blurbs. Obviously, this would not benefit you by using it in the proposal, but it would surely help sell the book by having them listed on the back cover. Talk with your publisher or agent about the best people they know and how to contact them.

When all else fails and your dream list does not come to pass, you can still fill in the endorsements page with people whose professions qualify them to comment, even if their names do not have instant recognition.

Consider the local bookstore manager or your state senator. How about a local psychologist or minister for your self-help book? Try local chefs at fancy restaurants for your cookbook. Be creative when rounding out your list. People will be honored to be asked, and probably slightly embarrassed if they are not famous.

Do not stop once your book is published. You are then a published author and have even more ground to stand on to ask people. In fact, you may want to go back to those people who said no and ask again.

You or your publisher may have chosen to list the endorsements in the front of your book. Remember that as your book is reprinted (because it is selling so well), you could always add new blurbs or replace the lesser ones with your better, late-addition people. It is well worth the expense to add these higher-quality blurbs into the book if it will catch the attention of a greater number of readers.

You are making great progress. Now it is time to get a publisher.

Chapter 23

Signing a Contract: Success!

Action is the foundational key to all success. —*Pablo Picasso*

PUTTING YOUR EFFORTS TO WORK

You have written some sample chapters, or perhaps the whole manuscript. You have a list of publishers or agents. Plus, you have created a dynamic book proposal and query letter. And you have some great endorsements. Now it is time to pull everything together and get published!

The most important parts of the remaining process are patience and perseverance. You may land a publisher quickly, but it's better to expect a long haul. Book publishing has many positive qualities, but lightning-quick decision making is not one of them.

Check your list of agents and publishers one more time. Prioritize them with your best match being at the top. Then, do one more read and grammar check of your query or cover letter and book proposal. Time to hit the send button.

While you wait, concentrate on your Author Promotional Platform (more on this to come). Or if you only have a few sample chapters, you might focus on writing your book. If, however, you have a final draft, do not continue to tinker with it. If you went through all the steps and have your manuscript in its best form, your time is better spent on other tasks.

While you wait, be prepared. Your most likely outcome will be no response. Or you will get a "not for us," which you will read as a reject. Expect these and therefore you will not be disappointed.

The time will come, however, when you get a publisher interested. It may be via an agent, or directly. But if you work the process and have a solid idea *and* have patience, you will see light at the end of the tunnel.

THE PUBLISHING CONTRACT

When you have a company interested, you will eventually come to an agreement on the project, and then you have a publisher! You have cleared a big hurdle. There is one important detail to wrap up before you pop the champagne: the contract. It is not official until you have received the contract, reviewed and understood it, signed it, and the publisher has countersigned it and returned a fully-executed copy to you. Prior to that, a publisher could have said yes but gotten cold feet and reneged on the promise. So, when the contract arrives, get a cup of coffee, sit down, and get ready for an education.

If you do not regularly review legal documents, looking at a book contract for the first time can be an imposing task. The contract will be anywhere from five to twenty pages in length. Many of the items discussed cover the same concepts from publisher to publisher but with different wording.

The contract is a necessary and important step. It spells out the conditions under which your book will be published. If all goes well, you will put it in a safe place and will never need to refer to it again. If things do not go as planned between you and the publisher, it should give you some understanding of your options. The contract is all about hypothetical situations, or "what-ifs."

Many people will fall back on the statement that they do not understand legalese. Most people, however, who are able to write a book are more than intelligent enough to read and understand the concepts included in a standard publishing contract. If you do not understand what is being said in the contract: ask, ask, ask.

Read through the contract one time. Take your time and think about what concept each clause is addressing. Each clause is probably included because of some previous misunderstanding between an author and a publisher. Your goal should be to understand every clause and its intent. Do not sign the contract until you can explain it to someone else.

The standard book contract favors the publisher since they wrote it. If you are a first-time author, it will probably be even more favorable to the publisher. It favors them legally as well as financially. If this does not sit well with you, perhaps you need to consider self-publishing.

Most of the contract is boilerplate or made up of standard wording. The publisher will add your name and address, book title, manuscript due date, and other variables to your version. There is not that much that changes in most contracts, and not much of substance you can negotiate if you are a first-time author. Publishers on average do not significantly revise contracts because the industry sees this as a perfunctory task in the publishing process.

The publisher's success comes from all of the books it publishes, not one specific project. If you doubt whether you are getting the best deal, ask the publisher if what it is offering is what most authors receive. If not, have the publisher explain to you why it is different for you. Most publishers will be honest and explain any differences to you.

Many first-time authors, with or without agents, worry about being made a fool of by blindly signing the contract. Many will consider consulting a lawyer. Most contracts are composed of standard wording with little leeway for changing the big or key points. Hiring a lawyer can be an expensive way to have it explained to you. If you do want to consider hiring a lawyer, do so for peace of mind, not with the expectation that you will get a tremendously better deal. If you do decide to get a lawyer, make sure they specialize in publishing or intellectual property. The lawyer who drafted your will or who lives next door will probably not be qualified. If you hire a local lawyer *not* familiar with publishing, you will be paying for them to get educated in the area of intellectual property and will probably not get much in the way of significant results.

Lawyers serve a valuable purpose in the publishing system. First-time authors, however, have little to no leverage. Know what the expenses for a lawyer will be before you sign on with them to review your publishing contract.

UNDERSTANDING ROYALTIES

There are some concepts that authors should be familiar with. Royalties can be calculated in many ways. Royalties can be calculated on the list price (which is the price listed on the cover) or on the net sales (that being after the publisher gives a retailer a discount). Being paid on the list price is obviously much more enviable but being paid on the net sales (especially for first-time authors) is much more common.

Average royalties for hardcover books might start at 10 percent, and trade or mass-market paperbacks might start at 8 percent. This varies only slightly from publisher to publisher. You could receive escalated royalties, meaning the percentage goes up as the number of copies sold increases. For instance, if you sell between 1 to 5,000 copies, you would receive 10 percent, from 5,001 to 10,000 you would receive 12.5 percent, and finally 15 percent for everything above 10,000 copies. Once the publisher has recovered its initial costs, you should share in the wealth. Always, always, always ask for escalated royalties. If they are there already, ask for greater escalation.

An advance is an up-front sum of money that the publisher is willing to give you to commit to the project and to submit an acceptable manuscript. Once the book is published, it will start to earn royalties, and these will work off the advance (but make sure to confirm this). After the advance is earned, further royalties will be paid if the book sells beyond the amount already advanced to you. Most likely, the publisher will not ask for the money back if the book does not earn back the advance (ask if the contract does not specify this). The publisher will try to give you an amount they feel comfortable the book will earn in its first one or two years. This may be the only money you ever see from the book. It is a common fact repeated by publishing insiders that many books in the trade arena never earn back their advance.

There may be items the publisher will charge back to the author's royalties. Examples include an index, permissions fees to use copyrighted material, illustration costs, and other items. Make sure it is completely spelled out as to who is responsible for what items. You will probably be paid your royalties once a year. If possible, ask for them to be paid twice a year. Also, if you are to receive an advance for writing the book, the contract should specify when it will be paid (for example, upon contract signing, at manuscript submission).

The contract will contain details like who owns the copyright and publishing rights to the book. The copyright states who created the material. Copyright exists when the material can be shown to have first been created. Copyright is later registered with the Library of Congress. The copyright for the book may be registered under the publisher's name or under the name of the author. The publishing rights, however, will need to be signed over to the publisher. This gives them the right to make the material commercially available. The publisher will obviously need these rights to make your material available to its customers. Someday when the work goes out of print (hopefully years from now), all rights will revert back to you from the publisher. Make sure this is specified in the contract.

Another area the contract covers is the rights or subsidiary rights. This means other applications or forms of your work, even if they seem far-fetched. This may include a paperback version (if the contract is for a hardcover book), film/television/dramatic rights, audio rights, first serial rights (having excerpts run in a magazine before publication), second serial rights (excerpts running after publication), book club rights, electronic rights, or international translation rights (to create foreign-language versions). The contract will specify who holds these rights and how money from these rights will be divided. For instance, the publisher may hold rights to translate the book into another language. It may negotiate with a third party to translate the book into Spanish for a $2,000 fee. You may receive 50 percent of this payment, and the publisher keeps the rest (Bond, 2018).

If you have an agent, it may be worthwhile to try to retain some of these rights for them to negotiate. Some publishers may not agree with this, specifically for first-time authors.

WHAT TO NEGOTIATE

If you feel the urge to negotiate with the publisher, ask about items that will benefit the book. Sure, you can try to get a bigger chunk of money, but when it gets down to firm requests, ask for things that will help the book and therefore benefit you in the long run. Here are some examples:

- Ask whether additional specific marketing and sales efforts can be made on the book's behalf.
- Ask to have expenses reimbursed. Sometimes publishers will more quickly embrace paying expenses such as research rather than just larger flat sums paid to you.
- Ask about including the right to review and/or approve the editing, cover, marketing copy, and promotional pieces (none of which you are guaranteed to be consulted on). Many publishers will reject your requests. At a minimum, your requests will alert the publisher to your interest in being involved with these tasks.
- Ask for more free copies, a greater discount on the ones you can buy after the book is out, or a greater discount on copies you might be purchasing prior to release.
- Ask for the publisher to pay for the illustrations or materials taken from other sources.
- Ask to have the contract specify when the book will be released. A common way of expressing it is that twelve months after the manuscript is accepted, the publisher will agree to have a final book, or the rights revert back to the author.
- Sometimes authors will be paid a lower royalty outside the United States with the idea there is added expense. For eBooks, ask that the royalty be the same amount or higher since there are no physical expenses whether in the United States or elsewhere. Make sure your contract details the physical specifications of your book. If you think it is a big, hardcover, glossy text with photos and the publisher thinks it is a paperback with just text, there is a problem. If it does not specify it, ask for it to be added. If the publisher will not commit to it, ask at least what plans it has so you can flush out any potential misunderstandings.
- The contract may specify something called a reserve for return. This is an amount held back for years to offset returns between royalty statements. Ask to have this eliminated or reduced.
- Sometimes publishers will pay a lower percentage for books sold in great quantity. This is under the idea that the big discount they give should affect both of you. Ask to have this struck from the contract.
- Make sure the contract specifies what geographic region and form the publishing rights cover (for example, worldwide or just North

America, all forms or just print rights). If it does not, think about what is in your best interest and have them specified (Bond, 2018).

Of course, if you have an agent, they should hold your hand through the process, negotiating for you on the points they know will be flexible. You will not get everything, but it does not hurt to ask. Now, buckle in.

Part IV

GETTING PUBLISHED

Chapter 24

Submitting Your Manuscript

Finishing a book is just like you took a child out in the back yard and shot it. —Truman Capote

THE LAST STEP TOWARD PUBLICATION

You have signed a contract and you are off to the races!

If you only have sample chapters, now is the time to get started on writing the whole book. Being mindful of the manuscript due date in your contract, start to go through the steps detailed earlier in this book. Come up with a complete outline, then a draft, and then start to edit the work. Check your references and add great graphics. Find reviewers who will give you honest feedback and then make the appropriate changes. Run that final grammar check and make one last read.

Now it is time to submit your manuscript. Most publishers will have strict details on the format for your manuscript submission. Read their requirements (file format, separate chapters, references format, style guide preferences). Follow them to the letter. If you have any questions, reach out to your assigned editor for clarification.

Some publishers will have a web-based submission system as compared to emailing your manuscript to your editor. This type of system will require you to adhere to such points as file type. The system will require you to register. You will receive notifications to confirm receipt as well as it progresses through the system.

Let your editor know when you have submitted your manuscript. Check in on the next steps and timeline. Check in with your editor as time progresses.

Your publisher will have your work reviewed and then move it on to the editing and page makeup process.

As previously mentioned, once you have submitted your manuscript, do not just sit and wait for the next steps. Continue to build your Author Promotional Platform. Truly dive into publicity and marketing.

Chapter 25

Understanding a Publisher's Review and Addressing Revisions

Twice and thrice over, as they say, good is it to repeat and review what is good. —*Plato*

WHAT IS A PUBLISHER'S REVIEW?

Your publisher now has your manuscript. Depending on your content and the subject matter, the publisher will likely have it reviewed. A publisher's review could describe different types of processes. It may mean your editor confirming the broad details of your work, such as agreed-upon page/word count, number of images, or format.

The publisher may, however, choose to send it out to content experts who will read the manuscript very closely and make comments. They may send it to just one expert or as many as three, four, or more. Each reviewer, with their own perspective, will give their comments and feedback to your editor. The editor will synthesize these and make a decision on publication.

Another type of review the publisher might seek is to show your work to members of the book's target market. They might read it less for details and accuracies but more to determine its interest to customers and whether they would buy it.

Whatever the extent of the review, your editor will give you a summation of the feedback. They will likely make a request for some (or more than some) changes. These changes might be with regard to grammar or structure. They might be to clarify references or citations. They could possibly be more extensive. They could involve condensing or expanding sections, which means rewriting. On the content side, the editor may give you some extensive feedback. The comments would likely be blind, meaning that the reviewers' names and credentials would be unknown to you. The comments may come as tracked changes in your manuscript or as a bulleted list of comments.

RESPONDING TO REVIEWER COMMENTS

Hopefully, the comments will not be overwhelming. If they are more than mechanical, read them carefully. Let them sit and come back to them later and read them again. Weigh them carefully. Be honest with yourself. The human reaction is to be defensive. You and your publisher have the same goal: a quality book that sells and is well received.

If you agree with all the points in the review, sit down and start to revise your work. If you agree with some but not all of them, then you will need to go back to your publisher. After your careful consideration, compose a response to your editor. Make a list of all the suggested changes you agree with. Then move on to the others. For some, you may be requesting clarification. Others may not align with your vision of your work or may not be in the best interest of the book. List those with which you do not agree. In an objective fashion, explain your position. Give details as to why they do not work for your book.

After you and the publisher have worked out which changes are to be made, get to work revising your manuscript. When you are done, run another grammar check. If you did extensive reworking or rewriting, you may need to go back to the editing phase including others reading your work, or you reading it aloud.

When it is in its final form, resubmit it to the publisher. Include a letter with the details of the changes you have made, noting the requested revisions. Write this letter in a neutral tone and without judgment. Things are moving along now.

Chapter 26

Accepted!

The true worth of a man is to be measured by the objects he pursues.
—Marcus Aurelius

OFFICIAL ACCEPTANCE

The publisher will receive your revised manuscript. They will need to review the work again. If the requested changes were mechanical or minor, your editor may review the changes themselves. If the changes were more extensive, they will send the manuscript back to the peer reviewers for them to reconsider it. They will likely provide your letter about the noted changes to the peer reviewer. This is the reason your note about your revisions needs to be objective and in a neutral tone. Your editor may translate your statements into their own words but there is a chance they will provide your actual letter to the reviewer.

At some point however the decision will be made to move forward with the publication of your book. The editor will be in touch with the good news. They will explain the next steps in the process. You will likely be assigned a different editor who will do the actual editing of your work. A different person or company will be assigned the layout of your book. Yet a different person may be assigned for creating your cover. You may have been in touch with the publisher's marketing department. If you have not been in touch with them, your editor will connect you with them at this point as well. The following chapters will cover all of these processes.

While your work is not over, you have accomplished a tremendous amount. You should pause and congratulate yourself for getting this far. You will have to review all of the publisher's work, but the real tasks ahead are the marketing and promotion of your book. Embrace this challenge. You can personally help assure your book's success and ensure that it reaches the right audience.

Chapter 27

Envisioning a Cover Design

Beauty is only skin deep. —*Anonymous*

THE IMPORTANCE OF THE COVER

Hands down, the cover of your book (along with its title) is perhaps the most important element in a book's success. Your publisher at some point may (should) let you know your cover is being designed. They should ask for any thoughts you have on it. Before signing the contract, you may want to discuss your vision for the cover. It will help to verify that you both see eye to eye on what the visual representation will be. Some potential authors even have a dummy cover created to submit with their proposal.

Will your cover be a soft focus with muted colors? Will it be bright and eye-catching? Will there be a photo, or a drawing, or just text? Will it smack you in the face or be very subtle? These are important aesthetic questions that dramatically affect the way your book is perceived. Be assured when you are working with cover creation that the old saying about judging a book by its cover exists for a reason. It happens with every book, every day. When you visit the library and bookstores to gather ideas and competitive intelligence, see how you are influenced by cover designs.

Be prepared for the conversation with your publisher about your cover. Write your thoughts down to help convey your vision of what your cover should look like so there is no misinterpretation.

Start out with the broad feeling that you are trying to convey. Give examples of graphics that might be appropriate. Examples of images you have or that you found online will help the cover designer understand your vision—the more specific and the more detailed the better. Hopefully, the publisher will see cover creation as a collaboration. In most instances, the publisher has the final say. Respect this and do not try to fight the system. Make your feelings well known and explain your rationale.

The more designs to consider, the better. If you are given various options, hang them up on a wall to ponder the differences. Do not make an immediate judgment.

Have your friends and family give their feedback. Look at the covers from five to six feet away. Is the title readable? Is the title visible when displayed in black and white? What does it look like when displayed postage stamp–sized on a laptop screen or on a smartphone? Cover up the words in the title and ask some people who do not know about the project what they think the book is about. See what message the graphics and design are sending the reader.

Compare it to the competitive books. Make sure that coincidentally you have not matched the design of another book which could lead to confusion.

Your cover will also include the spine and back cover which you should have an opportunity to review. The marketing text on the back cover is very important. Review it closely to ensure it sings.

As with the title, spend too much time on this step and give it your all. Some publishers may limit your involvement. They are the professionals, but you know your content and market better than they do. Take a positive approach and work with them as much as they will allow. Be open to their ideas.

Chapter 28

Reviewing Page Proofs
and the Final Steps

What appears to be the end of the road may simply be a bend in the road. —*Robert H. Schuller*

YOUR PART OF THE PRODUCTION PROCESS

When your manuscript has been accepted, the publisher's work starts. You need to remember that you have ceded control to the publisher. You will *probably* be consulted on changes or alterations. If you go into the process feeling that you have sent your child off to college for new experiences outside your control, then you will be in good shape. Any consultations that the publisher makes with you, if you have this frame of mind, will be a positive experience.

The traditional position has been that since the publisher spends all the money on production, printing, and marketing, it gets to have the final say on these topics. However, make it known to your publisher that you want to be involved in all stages of the book's production.

Follow up through the process to ask about the book's progress. Be positive and make sure you let the publisher know you are trying to help improve the quality of the book. Agree with them that they know publishing, but your feedback as an expert in this area will help improve the book's reception with its audience. Through the whole process, if you are unsure or do not understand something, ask, ask, ask.

One note—patience should be the order of the day (or year). Shock of all shocks, the publisher has projects to work on other than yours. Your book will be scheduled for a specific release date or season. The entire schedule works backward toward its release. Most authors feel it is not quick enough, but you will need to have patience.

When the publisher receives your manuscript, it will be assigned to an editor. This editor may be an employee or a freelancer. It is important to see your editor as an ally, not an adversary. They are working on your behalf to make your book a better product.

The editor will start with an initial read-through of the manuscript, making the first edits to your work. The editor will be checking for grammar, spelling, and punctuation, but also to make sure the material flows logically and clearly. They will want to ensure that the reader is getting their questions answered by the way you present the material. They may start to change or even rewrite sections. How much this is done will depend on the material, your authoring skills, and the publisher and editor. Some publishers may have you review files with their edits and tracked changes. Many will simply have you wait until it is typeset.

After the editing process, the next step will be typesetting or page makeup. The book will pass from the publisher to graphic designers or people responsible for making the edited manuscript look like the pages in a book. This page makeup process has evolved in just a few years from a complicated one, requiring specialized equipment and the expertise of someone with a technical background, to one that can be accomplished on almost any computer that has specialized and relatively easy-to-use software.

The result will be electronic page proofs of your edited final manuscript. It will look and feel like the real thing. The publisher should give you the opportunity to review the page proofs. This is probably your one and only chance to review the book in its edited and changed form. Set aside the appropriate amount of time to review it based on when the publisher needs the pages returned. Read the pages through to see how it has changed. Do not rewrite their changes to put them back the way they were. Ask about any changes or alterations and why the changes were made. Ask in a positive manner; do not make demands.

THE STEPS THAT FOLLOW

Note any corrections that need to be made. Keep a copy of the changes you have requested. After the publisher receives your comments, follow up and ask if changes were made, and if you will see another set of page proofs. Not all publishers will allow an author to see a second set. After the changes have been made, the publisher will probably review and reread the book one more time. Then it is off to the printer. If possible, get a copy of the final page proofs that the publisher sent to the printer. These pages virtually duplicate what the book will look like. The publisher will give you a target date of when you should be seeing an advanced copy. The only thing left in regard to production is patience—waiting for this date to arrive. The date you receive the first advanced copy is not the official release date. These dates may be separated by days, weeks, or months. The publisher times the official release date to coincide with a selling season or the book's availability to its customers or distributors.

The time waiting for the first copy will be no time to relax. All through the process of manuscript creation, and even prior to that, you will need to be busy with marketing and publicity.

The next chapters detail what should happen when selling the book, and most importantly, what role you can play. Marketing is the least understood part of the publishing process by most authors, yet it might just be the most important part of what an author can do to make a book a bestseller.

These activities will all need to be minutely orchestrated to coincide with the book's release. You may be contacting blogs or news sites, setting up interviews, arranging a party, or getting a website created.

All of your efforts—writing, editing, looking at page proofs, beginning marketing and publicity efforts—all lead up to one thing. You are days away from officially being a published author.

Part V

YOUR PUBLISHED BOOK AND THE IMPORTANCE OF MARKETING

Chapter 29

How a Publisher Markets and Promotes a Book

Everyone lives by selling something. —*Robert Louis Stevenson*

STARTING WITH BASIC TERMS

To be honest, these next two chapters are the most important in this book. But these chapters also might be the least read, least followed, or least understood. Marketing, sales, promotion, publicity, advertising, distribution—they all run together for most people. These terms, however, serve a separate yet harmonious role in spreading the word about your book.

If you are going the traditional route, you can (and should) play a part in marketing your book. You should also know exactly what your publisher will do (and not do) in this area. If you are self-publishing, marketing and promoting your book is squarely in your court. If you do not do it, it will not get done.

It is amazing that an author can write a 500-page manuscript and spend months revising the work. Then, many of these same well-meaning authors will doggedly avoid all promotional and marketing duties. Some authors feel they have done their part, and this is not their job. Others feel it is below them or unseemly for them to promote their own work. If they have these perspectives, then when their book disappears from the radar screen after six months, the author should not complain. If you do not want to take as active a role in marketing and promotion as you did in writing, you are missing opportunities to make your book a success.

If you are leaning toward self-publishing and want your work read and talked about, then closely read the next two chapters. If you do not feel that you can pursue the majority of the points discussed with enthusiasm, then reconsider self-publishing. Ralph Waldo Emerson said, "Nothing great was ever achieved without enthusiasm." Be not only the inspired writer but an active spokesperson/salesperson/marketer for your work. Inspiration sells and, yes, you need to be genuinely inspired!

Now, let us talk about what nuts and bolts are involved with letting people know about your book. First, review the definitions of these terms that may be the cause of some confusion to a novice:

- Promotion: Refers to letting your customers know about the book. It is a broad term that covers many types of activities. Most times, these efforts are time intensive and cost little or nothing.
- Publicity: Refers to the result of promotion when the media (and customers, depending on the context) find out about your book, with the result being exposure to other readers. Most times, these efforts have little to no cost, but they can have a high payoff when done effectively.
- Advertising: This usually refers to placing an advertisement on social media, through online ads with a platform such as Google, or in a magazine, newsletter, etc. The desired result will be for the customer to buy the book from you/online/at a bookstore or possibly to attend your speaking engagement (and buy the book). For clarity, advertising almost always comes with an expense attached to it.
- Marketing: A broad term that covers all of the formal activities of letting people know about the book. This may include writing the descriptive copy for the book, creating a direct mail or email, dealing with distributors/bookstores/libraries, etc.
- Sales: This term refers to actually talking to customers about your book. It may mean talking to just one customer at a presentation, or to a bookstore manager, or to a company that may buy the book in quantity. It means convincing one person that the book is right for their needs.
- Distribution: Refers to getting your books to companies that will put them in the hands of potential customers. These intermediaries may

distribute your book to online retailers, bookstores, libraries, or other retail outlets. This group may include distributors or wholesalers; they may be exclusive or not; and they may be regional, national, or international (Bond, 2018).

No matter which term, the goal of all of them is to get books in the hands of potential customers.

One of the first things that you determined was your market. What is the profile of people who will want to buy the book? What is their typical age? Gender? Educational background? Do they belong to any specific organizations or clubs? Do they subscribe to any special publications? Do they work in specific locations? The more you solidify who your potential readers or customers are, the easier promoting and marketing your book will be. Also, think of the keywords and make sure they are included in your marketing.

If you are going the traditional publishing route, you should have a clear idea of exactly what the publisher will be doing for your book, and how you can work with it. Hopefully, early on in the process (at contract-signing time), you and the publisher discussed specifics of their commitment. Perhaps you even got the publisher to put it in writing.

Even with this understanding, the publisher may change their commitment. As sales improve, it may do more. Conversely, if sales do not meet its expectations, it may withdraw promised efforts. It is basing many decisions on its entire line of books, not on just one. In any case, have a clear idea of responsibilities ahead of time. A face-to-face meeting (or video call) with the publisher about the book in general or just on the topic of marketing is ideal. This will allow your enthusiasm to spill over. It will allow you the opportunity to personalize your connection with the people who will be working on your book and to assess their commitment.

The actual list of what a publisher will do (or not do) will vary greatly from book to book, from topic to topic, and from publisher to publisher. You will need to adapt these options to your individual circumstances. If your publisher is not using one of these methods, that does not automatically mean the publisher is doing a bad job.

If you are going the self-publishing route, take note of all of these. Ideas abound!

HOW DO PUBLISHERS MARKET BOOKS?

The publisher may be responsible for:

- Making the book available through the major online retailers such as Amazon and many others. The book should be a stocked item and should be available for quick delivery. The publisher or its distributor needs to be on good terms with these crucial outlets. Also, all the information the publisher presents on your book needs to be comprehensive, complete, and include all favorable reviews.
- Making the book available in bookstores. The world has changed a lot for bookstores in the last ten years. Amazon has had a negative effect on brick-and-mortar bookstores, as has the pandemic. Independent bookstores are still around, and they are a godsend where they exist. Support them when you can. There are some specialty bookstores, as well as college bookstores, which might be ideal for your market. But the opportunities for sales in these stores or for speaking engagements are not what they used to be. The publisher will use a distributor to get the books into the stores. Its distributor may just take orders, or the distributor may promote the book. The distributor may call on all stores, just certain types, or only those in a specific geographic area. If your book is a specialized or technical one, it is more important that the publisher have the book in technical bookstores, as opposed to those in a mall. Beware, returns of unsold books plague the industry. Books that are "sold" to a bookstore can easily be returned. This is true for other avenues as well, but not to the degree as with a bookstore.
- Selling the book to libraries. The publisher will use a specialized distributor, a library distributor, to get the word out. Libraries are a great place to have your book and expose it to new readers. Some of these customers will eventually buy the book for themselves. Plus, if your book is worn because of use, the library may repurchase a copy or copies. Beware though—the digital revolution has been as disruptive to the library market as it has been to bookstores. Library budgets are lean and eBooks for many have not kept up.
- Providing sales support to university professors to make them aware of the book, if it might be used in a college course. When a course uses a book, it is called an adoption of that text. Most commonly, the

instructor is given a free copy of the book. Skimping in this area (if the book has a legitimate audience here) is foolhardy as this can be a low-cost, high-return effort. If your book is a textbook, working with a publisher on a knowledgeable, effective campaign to professors is the goal. Make sure you coordinate all efforts early on.

- Making copies of the book available at your presentations. These copies can fly off the table at successful speaking events. "Back of room sales" can be an important arrangement to have the publisher involved in. The books would need to be transported to the talk, sold, and the leftover books and receipts returned to the publisher (or you). Of course, the pandemic made a dent in this market. Consider creating a coupon that you can distribute after your talk (in person or virtual) that allows people to remember the book title with links on how to order it.
- Making digital or paper fliers available to you for any of your presentations. The flier should have a description, copy of the cover, and complete ordering information (website, phone number, address). The flier should also have a promotional code that can be tracked to see how many people order off of it.
- Providing a copy to appropriate blogs, websites, or newsletters for review. These copies are sent free and may be sent out prior to the book being released. These media outlets are some of the best sources of publicity for the book. They can be found with relentless searching online, as well as by networking with other writers and authors.
- Contacting blogs, websites, magazines, or newspapers about publishing a story or post that involves the topic of the book. Of course, your article, and the blurb at the end, would reference the book and how to order it.
- Arranging for podcast, video channel, or radio/television interviews. Talk to your publisher to honestly assess your chances here. Perhaps your opportunities are limited by your specialty topic. Essential to any interview is to have the books at online retailers. If the customer looks online and cannot easily find it, they probably will not come back.
- Including the book in the publisher's seasonal or yearly catalog. This catalog will be used in several ways, such as sending out information to its distributors or best customers.

- Creating an email campaign to the publisher's best customers to let them know about the book. Perhaps it can offer a 20 or 30 percent prepublication discount to develop preorders. Or the publisher could rent email addresses for a very focused group.
- Creating an advertisement to run in a magazine, newspaper, or newsletter about the book. This is extremely rare because of the economics. Selling $25 books one at a time via an ad is tough. If you are writing in a specialized market, there might be specialty or trade publications that work, but this is doubtful.

To reiterate, no publisher will do all of these items on every book. Most times, the individual market will dictate what is accepted practice. It is best to talk with your publisher and find out what it will be doing and not doing in these areas.

WHAT TO ASK YOUR PUBLISHER

Having read all of the possible activities a publisher might do for your project, here is a list of questions to ask before you start to work together. There are no right or preferred responses. What is right for your book will depend on the publisher and the market. Do not be afraid to ask or make requests of the publisher. Unfortunately, the publisher has a lot to do, but the squeaky wheel does get the oil. Bearing in mind the bulleted items above, here are some questions to ask:

- Will my book be in bookstores? Do you have salespeople that call on buyers for bookstores? Will it be considered an in-stock item at Amazon?
- How will you let libraries know about my book?
- Do you have a website for people to purchase it?
- Will you be able to provide fliers for me for my own promotional efforts?
- What support do you give for speaking engagements?
- What are your general guidelines on complimentary review copies? How many can I expect to be sent out to podcasts, websites, blogs, or magazines?

- How will my book and the other titles you publish be marketed together? Will my book benefit from these efforts?
- Will it be available outside the United States? How and through whom?
- When will marketing and promotional efforts start prior to the book's release? How long after its release will it continue to receive active attention?
- Can I be involved with the creation or approval of the marketing materials for the book?

See the publisher as your partner not your adversary. Work with them to ensure wide distribution (and sales) of your hard work.

Chapter 30

An Author Promotional Platform and Why It Matters

You have within you right now, everything you need to deal with whatever the world can throw at you. —*Brian Tracy*

YOU ALREADY HAVE A PLATFORM AND MAY NOT KNOW IT

What is an Author Promotional Platform? It is the name that the industry and publishers have used to define the author's ability to find and communicate with their audience. It has gained in prominence so much that in recent years, publishers and agents will consider it of primary importance (along with the book idea and author's background) when deciding whether to commit to a project or not.

You cannot ignore this concept. You have a platform, whether you think you have one or not. You communicate with colleagues and coworkers. You understand your market better than your publisher. You read about your subject at websites, attend meetings, and are generally immersed in it. Now you just have to see yourself as having an Author Promotional Platform and be enthusiastic about putting it to use to promote your book.

Create a Marketing and Promotional Plan for your part. List the items you know you can do and others you would like to attempt. List them by category, with all of the ones dealing with speaking together, and so on. Later, you can create a timeline of what needs to occur when. This plan is a living, breathing document that will change as time progresses. Keep it nearby. It will be your road map to success.

A LIST OF IDEAS

Here is a list of some activities that might be appropriate for your area (remember, not all of these activities will fit all topics):

- The number one goal is to expose the book to people who will have a fairly high level of interest about it. Whether accomplished through talks, or writing articles, or interviews, or meeting bookstore managers, it comes down to personal efforts. Think of who might be interested in your book and think about where those people can be found.
- Speak to groups diverse in interests. Find local organizations, clubs, or civic groups that might be receptive to your book. Is it a professional book? Speak at as many regional and national meetings as you can. Refine your speech. Make it one that people will remember and one that they would refer to other groups. Whatever you do, speak, speak, speak. Of course, the pandemic has changed this, but opportunities still exist. Make people know about and become interested in you and your book. Keep a copy to make notes in after each speech with regard to what gets asked about that is not in the book. When a listener asks you questions or makes comments, this is the best way to start to prepare for the next edition.
- Try to arrange a talk on your topic (or give a reading) at local venues or bookstores. Sign books and revel in the spotlight. Try to make your time at the bookstore a talk on the topic of your book more than a signing event. Would you rather have me sign your book or go to a talk on how you can write a book? An important note for book signings or talks: take a backup copy of everything. Bring a box of books, a poster, fliers, pens, maybe even a portable microphone. Like the saying goes, "Be prepared." Scout the location and layout ahead of time. Assume that what can go wrong will. You will be happy you did. Bring business cards and bookmarks that have your order information. Business cards will help people remember the title of the book. Or create and print bookmarks, which are a great marketing

device. Leave a sign-up sheet for people to get on your mailing list. Then send people information about the book.

- Promote through social media. This step needs to start months and months before publication. LinkedIn, Facebook, Twitter, Instagram, TikTok, and others all are possibilities depending on the topic of the book. Gather followers/friends. Comment and connect with everyone and other authors. Pick one or two channels and really dive in. See how other authors use the channel. Important: when your book is released (and prior to it), the best posts are not, "Buy my new book!" Post about the content. Give excerpts. Relate it to what is in the news—anything that raises awareness. Social media is an essential tool for authors, and self-published ones in particular, to promote their book.
- Speak at libraries and make friends with librarians. Most medium- or large-sized libraries will allow you to present to their patrons. Many will allow you to sell books afterward. Give a talk on the topic of your book. Regional library systems can have significant buying power and getting to know the person responsible at the main office (either in person or by sending a free book) can lead to good things in regard to sales and publicity. Whether speaking at bookstores, libraries, or other groups, make sure these engagements are well-advertised and therefore well-attended. At the end, ask for referrals to other possible venues.
- Get as much local or national media coverage (podcasts, websites, blogs, magazines) as you can. When the book is about to be released, contact all appropriate media outlets. Do not ask them to promote your book; tell them you have a great story idea and get them excited about it. If the story will be in interview form, be prepared to explain your book in three sentences, five maximum. The simpler the better. During the interview, refer to your book by title at least three times.
- Have your own website, preferably using your name. The site can be simple, containing information about you, the book, a sample chapter, the table of contents, a way to contact you, and information about your speeches and presentations. Of course, you will want a way to sell the book online. The more free material connected to your topic that you can post at your site, the more likely that customers will return and perhaps buy. Provide a link to your publisher's website for the customer to make the purchase, or better yet, list links to the

online bookstores that support you the most. If your name is taken as a URL (for example my name, John Bond, was already a site), then try something else, like www.booksbyjohnbond.com. In the age of low-cost web technology with easy setup, there is little reason for each person not to have their own website! Do not delay.

- Build a mailing list of interested people. Some websites allow you to capture contact information of interested individuals. Or gather it the old-fashioned way at events or each time you contact someone. This list becomes invaluable when letting people know your book has been released or to publicize new events or other marketing opportunities.
- Mention your book in all your communications. When you email someone, have your email signature include the book title and website address. This allows you to remind everyone about your book each time they receive an email from you.
- Use those quotes. You worked hard on those endorsements. Hopefully, you got some more once the book was published. Also, reviews might be coming in from various publications. Put them to maximum use. Here are some examples: display them on your website, create a sheet of the best ones to be displayed at your talks or signings, quote them in any letters you send out about the book, add the best one to your email signature, add them to Amazon and innumerable other places.
- Author web pages. Well in advance of your book, sign up for a Goodreads account. Follow other authors. Add friends. Add reviews of books you read. When your book is published, make sure it is listed there and attached to your account. Connect, connect, connect. When your book is released and available at Amazon, claim your author page. Add bio, marketing info, and a photo. Maximize what you can with your page.
- Consider creating a short promotional video or trailer for the book. The technology is not a concern if you have a smartphone. Write out what you will say and practice it. The shorter the better. The video can be posted at YouTube (with a link to Amazon or your website), at your Amazon Author page, and at your website. People love short videos more than promotional texts. Be enthusiastic.
- Be a blogger. This can be very beneficial to your marketing, assuming you have a fair number of followers. The blog can follow your

creation of the book from writing to publication. Make sure the blog and book are tied together.

- Consider using a publicist. They are surprisingly affordable on a per project basis and can make connections more quickly, generating a lot of opportunities that might take you a long time to develop (Bond, 2023b; 2021a).

Be aware that many of these items start before manuscript creation. Some can continue to occur well after publication. They need to be carefully timed for maximum effectiveness. Also, there are many good books about online marketing, and how to get publicity. Some are listed in the bibliography, or you can go to an online bookstore and search.

Tirelessly devote yourself to promoting and marketing the book. The bibliography contains some books to read, and the resources contain pertinent websites.

Keep marketing long after the publisher has moved on. Spend as much time implementing the ideas in these chapters as you spent on creating the rest of the book. Work at promotion like this is what makes or breaks the book, because it will. If you worry that your book will end up being unknown and not bought by anyone, your efforts in this area can help prevent this. Try to do one thing each day to let people know about your book.

Chapter 31

Pursuing International Editions

There's the whole world at your feet. —*P. L. Travers*

HOW WILL YOUR BOOK BE AVAILABLE TO THE WORLD?

"My work will have broad appeal in Europe."
"China is a growing market and I think they'd love my book."
"I'd like to see a Spanish-language version of my textbook. It would be a hit."

Authors speculate on the market for their book outside of the English-language and/or North America. But what is involved with having your work reach Asia, Africa, Europe, and beyond?

Most authors sign a book contract with the idea of having the work published in English in the United States or Europe. But the majority of publishers secure all rights, worldwide, and in any language or format. Assuming this is the case for you, how can people get your book outside the United States and in their native tongue?

First, your publisher may make the English-language paper book available through a distribution agreement with a local book distributor or publisher. They in turn sell it locally. Of course, companies like Amazon, either through a regional version of the website (Amazon

Germany) or customers using the US site, could buy your original book and have it shipped to them.

Your publisher might also create an eBook and make it directly available outside the United States or through local or regional eBook platforms or resellers. This version would be in English.

The publisher might also pursue a translated version of the original work (Spanish, Mandarin, Japanese, for example). The publisher will start with contacting, directly or through a rights agent, a publisher in that region that specializes in that area (trade or mass market, medical, legal, etc.). The country counterpart will review the book description, market, sales figures, etc. and then request a sample print or electronic copy. Then they will review (or ask their industry contacts) to determine if it would find a place in that region of the world. If the publisher in that region wants to proceed, they would sign a contract to translate your work into their local language, have it typeset locally, and then publish a paper or eBook in their markets.

The payment for such an arrangement may be a one-time lump sum, a royalty, or both. The publisher would take a cut and the author would receive the balance. The author and the US/English-language publisher may put some conditions on the publication but, by and large, the regional publisher is in the driver seat since they know the market and the language. The author should receive a copy of the paper book, a proud day for any author. If the author has contacts in that area or will be speaking there, it is vital to let that regional publisher know (via the original publisher).

Expect little in regard to actual payment and royalty, and at most, you will be pleasantly surprised. These payments are usually icing on the cake compared to your English-language sales. For many geographic areas, publishing is less prosperous at lower price points. And the money is shared between more players.

HOW YOU CAN HELP

Having a person/colleague volunteer to translate your work is *not* the normal route to having this happen. You need to have that regional publisher interested in it as a commercial venture. Most times the publisher finds their own translator, one they know by the quality of their work.

What is helpful is to have a well-known figure in that region (and in that specialty) write a letter of endorsement for the work and its applicability or interest in that area. These letters will provide powerful persuasion to a publisher to consider translating and publishing your work.

A side note, large publishers may have regional/affiliate offices that might independently consider publishing a translated version. It is not a given, but they would go through the same process.

Talk to your publisher about the possibilities of an international edition and see if you can help in any way (Bond, 2021b).

Chapter 32

After Publication: Continuing the Journey

Wherever you go, go with all your heart. —*Confucius*

SEEING THE FIRST COPY

The UPS delivery person knocks at your door. Or you have received an email notification that the upload of your monograph is now available as an eBook. This is the payoff—the moment of truth. You rip open the box. There it is. It is even better than you imagined. Now it is official. You are a published author.

You have been working to set up speaking engagements about the book. You have interviews lined up. Your website has launched, and people actually visited it (other than you). The publisher's promotional efforts are underway. The distributors are excited about the book. They are spreading the word.

You can just hear the sales being rung up. Enjoy this moment. Make the best of it because there is still a lot to be done.

Think of today as January 1st. A new year has begun. A new chapter in your life, as you are now a published author.

WHAT TO DO NEXT

Here is a to-do list:

- Take one day for yourself. Relax. Call your friends and family and tell them the news. Brag, but in a nice way. Put your feet up. Enjoy the day, as there is a long and fulfilling road ahead.
- Make a resolution to use this new aspect of your life to its fullest. When you send emails, use the book and its website as your email signature. Mention it to new people you meet. Talk about it in your speeches. Carry it with you wherever you go. Give copies as gifts.
- Realize that you are an expert. Book publication confers status upon you. How much you believe you are an authority will subconsciously be transmitted to others. Use this elevation in a positive, productive way.
- Give yourself a party. Whether you call it a book signing, a launch party, or something else, it will help spread the word about the book. Perhaps you can get publicity for the party. Make it all work for you. Take pictures and post online.
- Gulp: start to think about your next book. Your next book will be much easier. You have invented the wheel and understand the process so much more. Think of your first project as the guinea pig. Remember, you are now an expert, not only in your field but in publishing. Maybe not an expert in publishing—but you are more of a veteran than most everyone you know. When thinking about a second project, consider quite a bit of the road already paved by you. Perhaps use the same agent, publisher, or promotional efforts.
- Remember that marketing and promotion need to be happening all the time. Make a vow to not become complacent. Stay in touch with the publisher over what you are doing, and more importantly, what they are doing. Right after publication, you may need to stay in touch every other day or thereabouts. After a while, continue to talk to the publisher, perhaps once a week.
- Stick to the Marketing and Promotional Plan that you created. Add items or alter others as things evolve. You should continue to consult the plan and add to it as time goes on.
- Start a campaign to add to your testimonials and endorsements. Now that your work has become an actuality, more people will probably

be willing to look at the book. Ask people who said no already, or people who did not answer. Now you can start your letter, "You may have seen my recently published book . . ." These new blurbs can be added to future printings of the book, or to your website, or to promotional materials. Think big and do not be afraid to ask, especially since you are a published author.

- Speak, speak, speak. Find groups that are appropriate to your area and talk to them. Display books or fliers. Take every opportunity to talk about the book.
- Send copies of the book to influential people in the field. Of course, you can ask them for an endorsement, but you also want to let them know the book exists. Ask them if they have any suggestions for spreading the word about the book. They may even end up mentioning it to some other important people as well.
- See your new accomplishment as a fundamental change in your background. You have a new career (or part-time career). Adjust your thinking and priorities.

Congratulations on your hard work and perseverance. You should be proud of your accomplishment. Whether it has to do with marketing or possibly keeping the book up to date via a new edition, think of the process as one that does not end. It is not a fifty-yard dash. It is not even a marathon. Think of it as a lifelong commitment. If done right, the package that you just received should not be a blip on your radar screen. It should continue to reverberate for years to come.

Sample Form

Publication Plan		
Task	*Target Date*	*Actual Date*
List your goals for you and your book.		
Identify your book idea or topic.		
Create a title and brief description.		
Identify your target market.		
Decide on solo authorship or find a coauthor.		
Create a plan and timeline for the project.		
Decide whether you will write the whole book, then seek a publisher. Or find a publisher/ agent, then write the book.		
Create chapter outlines.		
Write the first draft of the whole manuscript.		
Add figures or tables.		
Finalize references.		
Edit the manuscript.		
Review the style manual in your field for compliance.		
Have the draft of the manuscript reviewed by your friends, colleagues, or potential customers.		

Task	Target Date	Actual Date
Make appropriate revisions to the draft based on feedback.		
Choose between traditional publishing and self-publishing.		
If traditional publishing, decide between finding an agent or publisher.		
Do research and develop a targeted list of agents or publishers to contact.		
Create a quality book proposal and query/cover letter.		
Secure a publisher by signing a book contract or start the self-publishing process by finding partners to assist where needed.		
Get endorsements for your book.		
Submit your final manuscript to the publisher. Await reviewer comments and final acceptance.		
Review page proofs and cover designs from the publisher.		
Understand and support the publisher's efforts to market the book.		
Early in this process, start to create your Author Promotional Platform. Continue to grow and implement it to book launch.		
Book Publication!		
Continue your work to market and promote the book.		
Start writing your next book.		
Customize this plan and add details and target dates!		

Courtesy of John Bond, https://www.publishingfundamentals.com

Further Reading

Bond, John. 2018. *You Can Write and Publish a Book: Essential Information on How to Get Your Book Published.* West Deptford, NJ: Riverwinds.

———. 2021a. "Your work and international markets." Textbook & Academic Authors Association. September 9, 2021. https://blog.taaonline.net/2021/09/your-work-and-international-markets/

———. 2021b. "The What, Why, and How of an Author Promotional Platform." Textbook & Academic Authors Association. December 14, 2021. https://blog.taaonline.net/2021/12/the-what-why-and-how-of-an-author-promotional-platform/

———. 2022a. "Listen to Yourself." Textbook & Academic Authors Association. August 11, 2022. https://blog.taaonline.net/2022/08/listen-to-yourself/

———. 2022b. "Talk to Me: Using Dictation Software to Write." Textbook & Academic Authors Association. September 15, 2022. https://blog.taaonline.net/2022/09/talk-to-me-using-dictation-software-to-write/

———. 2023a. *The Little Guide to Getting Your Journal Article Published: Simple Steps to Success.* Lanham, MD: Rowman & Littlefield.

———. 2023b. *The Little Guide to Giving Poster Presentations: Simple Steps to Success.* Lanham, MD: Rowman & Littlefield.

Bibliography

Boice, Robert. 1990. *Professors as Writers: A Self-Help Guide to Productive Writing*. Stillwater, OK: New Forums.

Goodson, Patricia. 2012. *Becoming an Academic Writer: 50 Exercises for Paced, Productive, and Powerful Writing*, 2nd ed. Los Angeles: SAGE.

Heard, Stephen. 2016. *The Scientist's Guide to Writing: How to Write More Easily and Effectively throughout Your Career*. Princeton, NJ: Princeton University Press.

Herman, Jeff. 2023. *Jeff Herman's Guide to Book Publishers, Editors, & Literary Agents 2023: Who They Are, What They Want, How to Win Them Over*. Novato, CA: New World Library.

Herman, Jeff, and Deborah Levine Herman. 2016. *Write the Perfect Book Proposal: 10 That Sold and Why*, 3rd ed. New York: Turner.

Hofmann, Angie. 2018. *Writing in the Biological Sciences: A Comprehensive Resource for Scientific Communication*, 3rd ed. New York: Oxford University Press.

Kremer, John. 2016. *1001 Ways to Market Your Books, Real World Edition: Authors: How to sell more books, ebooks, multi-media books, audios, videos, white papers, and other information products in the real world*. Fairfield, IA: Open Horizons.

Lamott, Anne. 1994. *Bird by Bird: Some Instructions on Writing and Life*. New York: Anchor.

Literary Market Place 2022–2023, 83rd ed. Medford, NJ: Information Today, 2023.

Rein, Jody, and Michael Larsen. 2017. *How to Write a Book Proposal: The Insider's Step-by-Step Guide to Proposals that Get You Published*, 5th ed. Cincinnati, OH: Writer's Digest.

Strunk, William, Jr. 2020. *The Elements of Style*, 4th ed., New York: Pearson.
Turabian, Kate L. 2018. *A Manual for Writers of Research Papers, Theses, and Dissertations*, 9th ed. Chicago: University of Chicago Press.

Resources

PUBLISHING RESOURCES

Agent Query

https://www.agentquery.com/default.aspx

Book Marketing and Book Promotion

https://bookmarketingbestsellers.com/

Creative Penn

https://www.thecreativepenn.com/

Everyone Who's Anyone in Adult Trade Publishing

https://www.everyonewhosanyone.com/

Independent Book Publishers Association

https://www.ibpa-online.org/default.aspx

Jane Friedman

https://www.janefriedman.com/

Literary Market Place

https://www.literarymarketplace.com/lmp/us/index_us.asp

Publishers Lunch

https://lunch.publishersmarketplace.com/

Publishers Marketplace

https://www.publishersmarketplace.com/

Publishers Weekly

https://www.publishersweekly.com/

Query Tracker

https://www.querytracker.net/

Textbook & Academic Authors Association

https://www.taaonline.net/

Writer's Digest

https://www.writersdigest.com/

Writers Market

https://writersmarket.com/

Writing-World

https://www.writing-world.com/

SELF-PUBLISHING PARTNERS

AuthorHouse

https://www.authorhouse.com/en

BookBaby

https://www.bookbaby.com/

IngramSpark

https://www.ingramspark.com/

Kindle Direct Publishing

https://kdp.amazon.com/en_US/

Lulu

https://www.lulu.com/

Reedsy

https://reedsy.com/

Smashwords

https://www.smashwords.com/

Xlibris

https://www.xlibris.com/en

Index

About the Author

John Bond has been connecting with writers and readers for over twenty-five years. He is a publishing consultant. John founded Riverwinds Consulting in 2015 to advise individuals, publishers, and trade societies or groups on topics dealing with book, journal, and digital publishing.

Previously, John worked for a publisher, starting as an editor, and eventually became the publisher and then chief content officer. He has overseen the publishing of over 500 books and 20,000 academic articles in peer review journals in his career.

John is the host of the YouTube channel Publishing Defined, which provides brief informative videos on publishing. The channel has over 6,000 subscribers, and the videos have been viewed over 445,000 times.

He is a proud member of the Textbook & Academic Authors Association. In his prior career, John was a librarian in K–12 education and continues to be a strong advocate for libraries as an evolving place for learning and education.

John is the author of six books:

- *The Little Guide to Getting Your Journal Article Published: Simple Steps to Success*
- *The Little Guide to Giving a Poster Presentation: Simple Steps to Success*
- *Scholarly Publishing: A Primer*
- *The Request for Proposal in Publishing: Managing the RFP Process*

- *The Story of You: A Guide for Writing Your Personal Stories and Family History*
- *You Can Write and Publish a Book: Essential Information on How to Get Your Book Published, Second Edition*

Connect with John at Goodreads and see what is currently on his bedside table. He usually reads or listens to a book a week throughout the year.

John lives in New Jersey and owns more books than he will ever get to read but is trying.

Connect with John at his consultancy practice:
   https://www.riverwindsconsulting.com/
Find out about his work with individuals:
   https://www.publishingfundamentals.com/
See his other books at:
   https://www.booksbyjohnbond.com/
Connect with him on LinkedIn:
   https://www.linkedin.com/in/johnbondnj/
See any of his over one hundred videos on publishing on:
   https://www.youtube.com/JohnBond
Follow him on Twitter:
   @JohnHBond
Or email him at:
   jbond@RiverwindsConsulting.com